MY
sweet
MEXICO

—

Recipes for AUTHENTIC PASTRIES, BREADS,
CANDIES, BEVERAGES, *and* FROZEN TREATS

FANY GERSON

PHOTOGRAPHY BY ED ANDERSON

TEN SPEED PRESS
Berkeley

CONTENTS

ACKNOWLEDGMENTS

WHEN I BEGAN TO DO RESEARCH, I promised myself I would devote a section in one of my notebooks to recording the names of all the people I needed to thank. Not only did I not follow through on my own promise, but I also quickly realized I would need several notebooks to keep track of everyone.

Although the specific idea for this cookbook was planted a few years ago, my love for Mexican sweets began at a very early age. I want to thank my mother for teaching me as a child to appreciate the value in homemade food; she imparted her view of it as an art as well as showing me the enormous diversity we have.

I need to thank my sister, Yaelita, for always being my guinea pig and for being the person I imagined by my side while writing the book. To my brother, Jaisi Fus, for being a continuous source of inspiration and for never relinquishing his self-appointed personal cheerleader status.

The two most instrumental people to this book—who were truly vital to it coming to pass—are my dad and Manolo. Words cannot begin to express my enormous appreciation. They both helped me in so many ways—it's not that they don't deserve an individual acknowledgment, but rather that my gratitude is so immense that I wanted to thank them jointly. They made this book what it is by advising me as I organized my research strategy, housed me and my cats, encouraged me, pushed me, guided me, believed in me, and put up with a lot of samples and sticky floors! But most of all, I am thankful for their love, which has been present at all times—even when it forced me to dig deep to prove that this was my art.

This book is truly a collaboration involving friends, family, colleagues, craftsmen, strangers, and many, many people who love food as much as I do. I am very appreciative for their love and support.

I need to thank Lisa Queen, my agent, for pushing me to write the book I always dreamed of, for believing in me since the very beginning, and for her friendship. A big thanks to Eleanor Jackson who helped get things in order to submit the proposal and for her enthusiasm in the project.

If I created a publisher and hand-picked all of the people to collaborate with during the production of this book, I could never in my dreams have devised a better one than Ten Speed Press. Lorena Jones, although no longer part of Ten Speed, believed in the importance and passion of the book and I will always be grateful to her.

The uncanny patience that my editor, Melissa Moore, has had with me—dealing with my endless minute questions and my obsessive insistence to understand things—combined with her sensibility to Mexican food culture made her a perfect match as my editor. I feel very fortunate to have worked with her for many reasons and very happy to know that a friendship blossomed from the experience.

I also want to thank designer Katy Brown for putting all of the pieces together in such a lovely manner; I never imagined my book would look so good. And to photographer Ed Anderson, for helping me capture the essence of Mexican sweets and the people in such a beautiful and real way, as well as his patience in adapting to some unusual and unplanned travel circumstances. To everyone else at Ten Speed, my deepest gratitude for believing in the book as much as I do and for helping me make it happen.

There are many friends, family members, and colleagues that helped me along the way: some helped by guiding me or recommending a person or a place, others by showing me around and even giving me a place to sleep during my travels. I thank them all dearly but want to especially thank Roberto and Marco for letting me use their kitchen and their taste buds, for their input and ideas, but most of all for their unconditional support and love. They were there from the very beginning and even helped me guide my ideas—it has not gone unnoticed. I look forward to many more years of good food and friendship.

Shelley Wiseman will never know how much her advice on the process of recipe testing helped me out, but I hope to repay the favor someday! Jose Luis Curiel helped me obtain and understand many of the recipes that were hard to find and I will never forget the passion and knowledge he so generously shared with me.

Josefina is another dear friend and colleague that I need to thank for her support, advice, generosity, and introduction to her family, which helped enormously with many aspects of the book and beyond, as we have now become friends as well.

My friend Alex has looked out for me since I moved to New York a decade ago, always believing in me and the importance of this book. She has been a sort of guardian angel—I admire her professionally and personally, but most of all I feel fortunate to have her in my life.

Thierry and Maya are some of the most openhanded people I've met and they made the development of many of the recipes in this book possible. I am indebted to them and truly value their continuous encouragement.

There are always those "behind the scenes" people that make things happen without others ever knowing. In this case, I must thank Dado because I don't think I would've found the strength I needed to do the book without him.

Cristina Barros, Marco Buenrostro, Edmundo Escamilla, and Yuri de Gortari represent continuity and heart in the food history and culture of Mexico. They have inspired me and aided me in deepening my knowledge of the historical significance of recipes and ingredients and checking my accuracy, which is essential to the understanding and appreciation of our past and present.

I need to acknowledge authors Rick Bayless and Dianna Kennedy, who have educated people all over the world about the food and culture in Mexico for many years and have long been a source of admiration and inspiration for me. In a way, they paved the way for this book.

To all the kind strangers who guided me to unknown places, and to the different institutions, schools, government offices, casas de cultura, cab drivers, friends, friends of friends, anthropologists, street vendors, candy factory owners, bakers, crafstmen, and all the people who helped me retest the recipes—gracias!

Most of all, I have to thank the artisans that have kept the traditions alive through generations for their patience and love of the craft and for their delicious creations.

INTRODUCTION

SWEETNESS IN MEXICO IS FOUND ALL AROUND—in the intimacy of the home, at birthday parties, at patriotic holidays, during religious celebrations, and even at death. It's visible in the *capirotadas* (bread puddings) decorated with toasted peanuts, raisins, and *colaciones* (colorful hard candies) for Easter; in the chocolate and sugar skulls elegantly adorned with the names of mortals that don't scare anyone; and in the fragrant aromas of cooked guava and cinnamon for the *ponche navideño*.

The ubiquity of sweets may be true for many cultures, but Mexico's variety is something to be noted and celebrated. There are sonnets, melodies, paintings, and poems written about the subject; there are festivals and fairs; there are handmade sweets and breads made in the shapes of worms, pigs, corn, bows, ears, and shells. They are colorful and playful and embedded in our culture. It's a geography made up of *alegrías* (crunchy amaranth candies with nuts and seeds), *cocadas* (coconut candies), and *palanquetas* (brittles).

Mexico is renowned for sweet yeast breads that adorn the air with scents of cinnamon, anise, sugar, fruit, and honey; ice cream pushcarts that brighten the plazas and parks with watermelon, mango, and avocado flavors; and beautiful shops filled with confections that look like precious stones and taste like heaven (if it had a flavor)—if you haven't tried the bright green candied limes filled with sweetened coconut, the crumbly pecan marzipans wrapped in brilliant purple and orange papier-mâché, or the lusciously sweet goat's milk caramel hidden inside a round wooden box waiting to be opened like an engagement ring, then you haven't lived.

Mexico is a country that is privileged in the geographical sense. There are mountains, deserts, forests, coasts, and temperate rural areas. These provide an enormously diverse cuisine intimately linked and defined by the climate and products that are produced in each of them.

There are many candies, desserts, breads, and beverages that are associated with a certain region. The north of Mexico is characterized by candies made from milk, particularly goat's milk, and pecans; the roads leading to the coast have a wide array of coconut and tamarind candies; and the center of Mexico is known for its crystallized fruits, such as pumpkin, *chirimoyas* (custard apples), prickly pear, figs, and pineapple.

Even more distinct are the *pastes*, derived from the term "Cornish pastry" that the British brought in 1824 to Real del Monte in Hidalgo; sweet sticky *cajeta* sold in wooden boxes or jars from Celaya; burnt milk ice cream from the markets and stands in Oaxaca; *dulces de arrayán*, a delicious soft candy made from this tart and fragrant fruit from Jalisco; *rompope* (similar to eggnog) from the convents in Puebla; the anise-scented bread from Pomuch, Campeche; and *chamuco*, a beverage made from fermented red plums, sweetened with *piloncillo* from Puebla.

The distinction between candies or confections and desserts is difficult to describe in Mexican cuisine. The word *dulce* literally means "sweet," and it is used both descriptively and as a

general term for candies or confections. *Dulces* are often served at the end of a meal as what many would consider dessert. However, sweets in Mexico are enjoyed at all times of the day.

I have always had a special affinity for sweets. Growing up in Mexico City, my favorite place to visit was a store downtown called Dulcería de Celaya. It is a family-owned store that has been around since 1874. Even after visiting countless times, I am transported to an era that has only existed in my imagination. The windows, ceilings, tile floor, wooden showcases, glass jars, and lamps allow me to escape the incredibly noisy and busy city right outside. The showcases are filled with delicacies, and the hardest thing to do is not buy the whole store! Brittle *turrón* made from almonds and chocolate cut into triangles, covered with a thin rice wafer; square goat's milk caramels with pine nuts carefully placed to resemble a flower; and giant crumbly meringues were almost an obligation.

Mexican sweets are a highlight of my childhood memories. I used to select the candies and fruit to fill my sister's piñata, which we carefully crafted each year. I remember strolling downtown with my aunt Cucus on Sundays while deliciously sweet and tart tamarind juice dripped down my cheeks from the melted *nieve* (sorbet). A friend of my father's, Dr. Abdon, would visit from Puebla and bring delicacies prepared by the nuns—beautiful cookies that resembled the sun, with a creamy center made from pumpkin seeds, and *borrachitos*, vibrant red gummies filled with a drunken juice of sorts, were always part of the selection. I anticipated his visits with much enthusiasm and discovered my love affair with Mexican sweets at a very young age.

Dulces through Time

A book about Mexican sweets is truly an encounter with the country's fascinating history that covers five distinct periods. The rich tradition of sweets is one of the fortunate results of the *mestizaje*, or cultural blend.

Pre-Hispanics utilized maguey plants, mesquite, and insect honeys (such as ants, bees, and wasps) to sweeten things and turned out pumpkin seed brittles, amaranth candies, and beverages made from cactus and cacao. The presence of the Arabs through their ingredients and exquisite artistic sensibility impregnated Spain and was adored by Mexico; they influenced the marzipans, *buñuelos*, brittles, *conservas*, and fruit *pastes*.

The conquest by the Spanish of Tenochtitlan, the Aztec capital, began in 1521, and they brought with them more than just weapons. They arrived with cinnamon, wheat, cows, nuts, and sugar cane. The thousand or so nuns who arrived in Mexico gave life to an endless world of candy making. They supported themselves by making and selling confections and adapted their recipes to embrace tropical fruits, vanilla, corn, cacao, and new sugars. The importance of the religious convents as producers of sweets was fundamental in the New Spain.

The Spaniards' cuisine and culture was deeply influenced by eight centuries of Arab occupancy, and this was apparent in their use of preserves, tamarind, dates, spices, and overly sweet preparations that helped preserve food in the warm climate. Their arrival undoubtedly enriched our cuisine, and it is fair to say, in my opinion, that the combination of the imports from Europe and the indigenous ingredients of this land composes what we refer to as traditional Mexican cuisine today.

Sugar cane is perhaps the most influential ingredient that the Spaniards brought to the culture of sweets. Its introduction in the New Spain was only three years after the fall of Tenochtitlan in 1524. It is believed that Spanish conquistador Hernán Cortés ordered the first *trapiche* (a rustic sugar mill commonly fueled by water or animal strength).

In the first decades of the colony, candy was produced in four places: in the *trapiches* and *ingenios* (industrialized sugar mills) by artisans using the sugar mainly to make preserves and crystallized fruit; in the convents by the nuns; and by some home cooks and producers who sold their merchandise on a small scale.

In the sixteenth century, Sebastián Elcano arrived in the Philippines. This expansion of the Spanish throne opened new routes of commerce between two faraway lands that had not been in contact previously. As with Arab sweets, there is a parallel in flavors between these two lands that has remained apparent ever since.

Independence from the Spaniards occurred in 1810. At that time, the influence of French cuisine enriched Mexico's sweet culture with its napoleons, cakes, and ice creams. The French brought new techniques and styles of sweets, with an emphasis on those that were very rich, buttery, and creamy. Layered cakes, rich ice creams, and the way to enjoy sweets—moving from cloistered parlors to cafés and plazas—were just some of the francophone influences. The populist administration of Porfirio Díaz played a very important role in this shift, and the consumption of sweets became a more popular affair rather than an elitist one.

The inherited culture of the Revolution, a century later, allowed for the continuity of techniques that are deeply rooted in our culture, both popular and regional. Many of the desserts, breads, confections, and beverages have remained the same but introductions of new flavors can always be found, particularly in the enormous diversity of candies made or finished with spicy and/or very sour flavors. Fancy restaurants and shops continue to borrow techniques from the Europeans, while always putting Mexican flavors at center stage.

Today, however, many of these heirloom recipes are part of an oral tradition that is being lost. Younger generations are not as interested in these sweets or don't have the time to make them, and the heart of the older generation resists the uniformity of modernization.

In my quest to save these recipes from extinction, I visited artisans in small family-run factories, homes, museums, libraries, bakeries, ice cream shops, and endless markets. I talked to everyone I knew, everyone who might know someone who may know someone who has heard of someone in a place where it is said they make the best ice cream, bread, or caramel. I spoke to everyone I could, even when I was asking for directions or buying a bus ticket. The people working in the different *casas de cultura populares*, taxi drivers, and market vendors seemed to be some of the best resources. I was not always welcomed, because people are very protective of their recipes and many told me they prefer to go to their grave with them rather than share, even if no one in their family is interested in them at all.

On the other hand, many candy artisans welcomed me and showed me how their treats were made; some even gave me their recipes, for which I am extremely grateful. As a Mexican pastry chef, I then filled in the blanks, so to speak. Although I discovered many wonderful things along the way, my journey only reinforced the fact that there is still so much more to learn, to savor, and to document.

It is not surprising that one of the hardest things for me was to let go and not include some recipes. With more than three hundred types of regional confections and two hundred varieties of sweet morning pastries, not to mention the countless fruits in Mexico and new recipes I found along the way, the task was not easy. Many of the original recipes are very lengthy, so I have made them more user-friendly while preserving the essence that captures much happiness from my childhood.

I believe that documenting is continuity, and I have attempted to do just that. I hope to highlight some of the most important aspects of Mexican culture and the wonderful people who have helped keep the traditions alive. Welcome to the cultural and tasty journey of my sweet Mexico.

INGREDIENTS GUIDE

MOST CHEFS, INCLUDING ME, will tell you that much of the success of a recipe lies in the quality of the ingredients. Imagine, for example, making the lime tart (page 202) with that awful juiced stuff that says something like "fresh tasting" versus actually taking the little bit of time to juice some fresh limes. Even basic ingredients like flour, sugar, butter, and eggs can make a big difference. Try a recipe you like with a few different brands, making a mental note of the variation, and you'll quickly understand why we chefs sometimes go crazy over something like eggs.

You might be surprised to find that a lot of the recipes in this book are made with familiar ingredients. However, there are key ingredients that you may be unfamiliar with, so I've included some basic information about them to help you out. The more you know about your product, the better understanding you'll have and better outcome. Luckily, many of the ingredients that I used to have to bring back from Mexico are much more available in the United States now. I hope that you are excited to try out new products and discover new flavors.

Acitrón

ACITRÓN Candied biznaga cactus usually sold in blocks and used in many savory and sweet preparations. You can substitute it for candied pineapple.

AGUAMIEL Commercially known as agave nectar, this is the sap or sweet juice from the agave plant.

AGUARDIENTE Clear brandy made from fermented, distilled fruit juice.

ALMIBAR Syrup made from cooked sugar and water.

AMARANTH A cereal that has been used in Mexico since pre-Hispanic times, amaranth has played an essential role in many rituals and ceremonies. The Spaniards tried to eliminate its production, but they were only able to diminish it; it is still used today most commonly in the *alegría* candy. Look for the puffed amaranth that has already been toasted and store in a dry, cool area. It makes a wonderful and nutritious addition to granola or yogurt.

ARRAYÁN Small yellow- to green-shaded aromatic fruit with tiny hard seeds and a very tart flavor. They are often eaten covered with sugar and are used to make candies.

AZAHAR This is the little flower that blossoms in the lime or orange trees. The orange blossom water is used in a few of the recipes. Make sure you get a high-quality one and not an imitation because the flavor will not only be unpleasant and artificial but also a bit soapy. Store in a dry, cool area or refrigerate if you're going to have it around for awhile.

BAKING POWDER Made from baking soda, cream of tartar, and cornstarch. Use double-acting baking powder, which is the most common, for the recipes here. Baking soda releases carbon dioxide when it is combined with a liquid and some more when it is exposed to heat, helping batters rise and achieve a light texture. Store in a dry, cool area and sprinkle a little bit over some hot water to see whether it fizzes. If it does, it's still good; if it doesn't, you should throw it away.

BAKING SODA Baking soda produces carbon dioxide when it is combined with some kind of acid. It can be placed in a refrigerator to absorb strong odors. Store in a dry, cool area. It lasts a very long time.

BOLILLO This is a crusty white bread used to make *tortas*, a kind of Mexican sandwich, and other dishes, including the sweet *capirotadas*. Use any other crusty bread, such as a baguette, in its place.

BROWN SUGAR This is simply granulated sugar with some molasses added to it. The darker one has a stronger, more molassy flavor, which is why it is used in place of *piloncillo* when it can't be found. Make sure it is tightly sealed so it doesn't harden; if it does harden, put it in a tightly sealed bag with a piece of white bread and you'll have soft sugar once again in a couple of days.

BUTTER Be sure to use the unsalted kind because it will allow you to control the salt in a recipe; don't use low-fat or imitation butter. It's quite simple: the more fat, the more flavor (82 to 86 percent butterfat is a good indicator of high quality and should be used in recipes where you want to show off the taste and richness of it). Be sure to keep butter well wrapped so that it doesn't absorb other flavors.

CACAO BEANS The cacao is an oval-shaped pod that grows on a tree. When you cut it open, a white sweet and delicious flesh encapsulates many seeds, which are, in fact, the cocoa beans (there are 30 to 60 per pod). These are left in the sun to dry out so they can then be roasted and used to make chocolate. There are many different kinds of chocolates made from a combination of different cacao beans. The three main varieties are *forastero*, *criollo*, and *trinitario*. *Forastero* is most often used because it doesn't have any outstanding fruitiness or acidity, which makes it a good base that allows other flavors and characteristics to shine through. It is also more resistant to disease, unlike the *criollo* variety, which is more delicate to harvest and yields fewer beans but has an exquisite fruity, deep flavor that is highly priced. The *trinitario* is a blend of the two; it has a complex flavor but is easier to grow and maintain than the *criollo*. Both the *criollo* and the *trinitario* are used to define the flavor of a chocolate, providing a unique characteristic to a base made from the *forastero*, which helps provide consistency.

CAJETA A yummy, sticky caramel made from goat's or cow's milk that has been cooked down with sugar. It is often used in sauces such as *crepas de cajeta*, in ice creams, and as a spread (or if you're anything like me, eaten by the spoonful). The most common ones come in three main flavors: *quemada* (burnt), vanilla, and *envinada* (finished with some kind of liqueur). The commercial ones are usually thicker, stickier, and sweeter but more easily found.

CAL (SLAKED LIME) This white powder is used in construction and in sport fields, but also is used to soak dried corn, making it much more nutritious and softer; it is also used in the preparation of candied fruits, creating a sort of barrier or crust so the fruit doesn't fall apart during hours of cooking. You can find it in some hardware stores, pharmacies, or tortilla factories, but you can also get quicklime (calcium oxide) in some ethnic supermarkets or Mexican grocery stores. It looks like small rocks and must be dissolved in water (it will sizzle quite a bit). The liquid is then used to cook the corn or soak the fruit.

***CAÑA DE AZÚCAR* (SUGAR CANE)** The long green canes are sold in many markets and cut into small pieces for you to enjoy by chewing on the fibers that deliciously release the sweetness as they are bitten.

CANELA The translation of *canela* is "cinnamon," but Mexican cinnamon is of the Ceylon variety, which is much more fragrant and less spicy than the more common ones. I know this may not seem like a big deal, but it is. The Ceylon sticks are much softer than the uniform Cassia variety and look like they have layers that coil or wrap around each other. When buying *canela*, break off a piece of it. It should be very fragrant and a bit sweet. Use it whole and break it into 2- or 3-inch pieces, or grind a few of them in a spice/coffee grinder.

CHILES There are a few different types of chiles used in this book, and there is an immense array of them in Mexico. In the sweet world, however, there are a few things to keep in mind. Don't buy any canned chiles because they will have other flavors and will be salty. In fresh and dried chiles, the heat is concentrated in the little veins and seeds, so remove these if you are a bit concerned about the heat. If they are fresh you can always soak them in salted cold water to remove any more spiciness. Most stores carry a larger selection of whole dried chiles than the ground ones, but you can always make your own powders by lightly toasting them in a hot skillet for a few minutes on each side, pressing down a bit and making sure not to burn them because the flavor will turn bitter, then cooling and grinding in a spice/coffee grinder.

Canela (cinnamon), *Caña de azúcar* (sugar cane), Chiles

CHOCOLATE DE MESA Chocolate used for Mexican hot chocolate. It has a granular texture and is made with sugar, cinnamon, and, in some cases, almonds. You can find it around Mexico sold in blocks, tablets, or balls and prepared in a *metate*; you can find some decent brands such as Mayordomo, Taza, and Ibarra elsewhere.

CINNAMON AND SUGAR I like to use a ratio of ½ cup granulated sugar to 1 tablespoon freshly ground *canela*. But use it as a guideline and blend it to suit your taste.

COCONUT See opposite page.

CONFECTIONERS' SUGAR This is also referred to as powdered or 10X sugar. It is sugar that has been processed to a very fine powder; most brands have a little bit of cornstarch added to keep lumps from forming, but you should always sift it before using.

CORN HUSKS The most common use for these is to make tamales. To soften them, rehydrate them in very hot or boiling water until they're pliable. Look for ones that don't have any holes or evidence of bugs, and be sure to dry them well with a towel before using.

CORNSTARCH This is most often used to thicken and stabilize different preparations. Be sure to keep it tightly sealed in a dry, cool area.

CORN SYRUP This thick, sticky syrup is used mostly in the candy recipes, which helps them achieve a certain texture and finish.

CREAM OF TARTAR What exactly is this? Well, it's the acid that is formed from the scrapings of wine casks once they've fermented. A small amount helps stabilize egg whites and helps avoid crystallization in some cooked sugar preparations. It is not an essential ingredient, but it is very useful. Replace with a few drops of cider vinegar if you don't have any when whipping egg whites.

CREMA (CREAM) The cream in Mexico is more acidic than regular sour cream and is very similar to the tangy and rich crème fraîche. For these recipes, use one to replace the other or make your own by combining 1 cup heavy cream with 2 tablespoons buttermilk. Cover and let sit in a warm area until it has thickened (about a day), and then refrigerate for up to 2 weeks.

DRIED FRUITS A few recipes use dried fruit. Avoid buying precut dried fruits because they are less likely to be fresh and may contain sulfurs. Sulfur dioxide is used to retain the color, but it changes the flavor and can cause allergic reactions in some people. If you buy in bulk, be sure to taste to ensure freshness, and buy plump ones. Store in a tightly sealed bag or container.

DRY ACTIVE YEAST Yeast is basically a collection of tiny living organisms that converts starch or sugar into alcohol and carbon dioxide and becomes active once it comes into contact with liquid, allowing dough to rise. Fresh yeast is the preferred choice of many bakers, but it is highly perishable and hard to find in many places, which is why I choose to use the dry active kind. There is a regular kind and a rapid kind. Although the rapid kind will save you much time, I prefer to use the regular one because it allows the dough to develop more flavor and texture. You can buy it in envelopes or jars, but make sure you store it in a dry, cool area. If you decide to refrigerate it, make sure it's at room temperature before you use it.

Understanding Coconut

The coconut fruit grows in tall palm trees. It is a large oval shape with an outer shell that is green or brown. The outer layer is usually removed to export it, and what you most commonly find are brownish hairy rounds that encapsulate the wonderful coconut meat and juice.

There are a few recipes in the book that call for fresh coconut. Below are steps to make the task of cleaning a coconut easier, as well as descriptions of the derived products and some ways to substitute them when you don't have the time or the patience to deal with fresh coconuts.

Choosing a Coconut
Pick a coconut that feels hard, is heavy for its size, "sounds" when you shake it, and has no odor or visible water around the "eyes." These can be stored for several months in a dry area, although some people recommend refrigerating them.

Making Fresh Shredded Coconut
Preheat the oven to 325°F. Place the coconut over a towel with the three dots facing up. Pierce the eyes using a screwdriver, an ice pick, or anything

sharp. Drain the coconut by turning it upside down; strain and reserve the juice for something else or enjoy cold. This is coconut water and shouldn't be confused with coconut milk.

Place the coconut in the warm oven until the shell begins to crack (about half an hour). Remove from the oven and allow to cool slightly. Place it on top of a towel, tap it all around with the bottom edge of a knife or a hammer to help crack it open, and remove the outer brown skin using a paring knife or a peeler. Cut the coconut into pieces and grind in the food processor or shred with a grater. Store in an airtight container in the refrigerator for up to a week or freeze for 5 to 6 months. One medium coconut will yield about 3 cups of shredded meat.

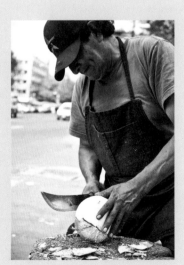

Making Desiccated or Dried Shredded Coconut
Preheat the oven to 250°F. Lay the fresh shredded coconut in a single layer on a baking sheet and place in the oven. Pay close attention so you don't burn it, stirring to make sure it dries evenly. Let cool and leave as is or grind in a food processor if you want it finer; store in an airtight container or a resealable bag (this can last for several months in a dry place).

Making Coconut Milk
Place the fresh shredded coconut in a blender, cover with very hot water, and blend until finely grated. Strain over cheesecloth and squeeze the coconut as much as possible. Discard the coconut meat. Refrigerate the coconut milk and use within 2 days.

To make coconut milk from desiccated coconut, repeat the same process as above using 1 cup unsweetened dried coconut and 2 cups water.

EGGS Eggs give structure to a lot of preparations, adding moisture and richness. In custards, for example, egg yolks, which are high in fat, thicken and enrich the milk and/or cream; egg whites, though low in fat, provide a lovely airiness and texture in many recipes. Nowadays, there are so many varieties of eggs that I am convinced they exist solely for the purpose of confusing us. I have used large eggs in all the recipes. Try to buy organic eggs from the farmers' market or from free-range hens. They will be more expensive than regular eggs, but they are better tasting and much fresher. Most recipes call for room-temperature eggs; this is because they whip up much better. You can either let them sit out for awhile or soak them in a container filled with very hot water for about 10 minutes; just be sure to dry them before you crack them. If you are separating eggs, it's easier to separate them cold and then let them sit, covered, until they are at room temperature.

***FLOR DE JAMAICA* (HIBISCUS)** The hibiscus is actually the part that covers the blossoms of the sabdariffa plant before they open. They are mainly used as an infusion to extract their lovely magenta color and tart flavor, and they are a natural diuretic. Look for deep-colored ones and store in a tightly sealed bag or container in a dry, cool area. You can find them in Mexican grocery stores, health food stores, or specialty teashops.

FLOUR To measure flour, be sure to use the scoop and sweep method, leveling it off with a knife, and sifting when indicated. It is best stored in a tightly sealed bag in the refrigerator or any dry, cool area. Note that some brands have a slightly higher gluten content, which will alter the thickness and consistency, so play around a bit with different brands to find one that you particularly like.

Flor de jamaica (hibiscus), *Guanábana* (soursop), Limes

GELATIN The two main forms of unflavored gelatin are the powdered form and the sheets. I have used the powdered ones for this book because they are easier to find and are less expensive with very similar results. Make sure you measure properly so that the texture is not too loose or rubbery.

GRANULATED SUGAR This is the main sweetener in the book. It is made from sugarcane or sugar beets, and either one can be used.

GUANÁBANA (SOURSOP) This fruit may seem a bit peculiar if you've never seen it. It has a green, thin, leathery skin with an extremely fragrant, creamy white flesh and large black seeds. It is quite hard to get outside Mexico, but you can find the pulp at many Latin or ethnic grocery stores or online. Make sure there are no added flavorings of any kind.

GUAYABA (GUAVA) Luckily, this fruit is becoming increasingly available outside Mexico. It is a very fragrant sweet fruit with small hard edible seeds. Look for ones that are yellowish and feel a little bit soft if you buy them fresh (the color of the flesh may vary from a yellowish to a pink tone). You can also get them frozen in many supermarkets or Mexican grocery stores. If needed, ripen in a paper bag for a few days, then store in the refrigerator until they feel soft but not mushy.

HEAVY CREAM Try to get heavy cream that has at least 36 percent milk fat because it is much richer and more delicious. It produces a smoother and thicker whipped cream as well.

LARD This is one of those ingredients that scare people away, but there are actually more reasons to love it than to hate it. Contrary to common belief, it is not "pork" tasting but has a neutral flavor, and it is one of the best fats to fry things such as *donas rellenas* because it won't penetrate the pastry and the flavor and texture will be much more pleasant. It adds a wonderful flakiness to many types of dough and toppings and a lovely silkiness to tamales. It actually has less saturated fat than butter and the natural kind has no trans fat, which means you must make sure you don't buy the hydrogenated kind! Leaf lard, the fat that surrounds the kidneys of a hog, is the preferred grade for baking, and fat back is the preferred grade for frying. The best way to get the good kind of lard is to render it yourself, which is actually quite simple. Ask your butcher or farmer for whichever fat you want to use and chop it into chunks. You can do this in a large pot over the stove, but I prefer to do it in the oven because it is less likely to burn. Put it in a deep pan with about ¼ cup water per pound of fat and bake at 300°F until it begins to melt. Stir occasionally until it has fully melted. You may hear something pop, and these are just cracklings. Once it has fully melted, strain through a fine sieve or a cheesecloth, discard the cracklings (or eat them), and refrigerate until solidified. Each pound of fat will yield about one pint of lard and will keep in the refrigerator for several months and in the freezer for about a year.

LIMES This is one of the main ingredients in Mexican cuisine. The most common variety is the Key lime or a small lime. Lime in Spanish is *limón*, which may confuse people because it sounds like lemon. However, we have very few of those yellow sweet ones in Mexican markets and kitchens. Look for smaller, bright green limes when making the zest and larger ones that feel soft for the juice, making sure you press it and roll it over a flat surface to loosen it and get as much juice as you can. Always rinse and dry very well before using them.

MAMEY This is an oval-shaped fruit with a light brown sandy shell. The flesh is a very creamy, lovely orange color. It is hard to come by, but make sure you buy some if you see them! Look for ones that feel heavy, have no indentations, and feel a bit soft when pressed but remain firm overall.

Mamey

MASA HARINA Literally translated, masa harina means "flour dough." It is sun- or fire-dried corn (different than the corn used for popcorn) that has been soaked in lime and water overnight to soften and "cook it," then rinsed and ground. Fresh masa is sold in many Mexican markets, but you can always use ground corn to prepare tortillas. (Maseca is the most common and widely available brand.) However, don't substitute it for other kinds of cornmeal like polenta because it is quite different in taste and texture.

MEZCAL Distilled liquor with a lovely, woody flavor made from a type of maguey plant. Avoid buying ones with the worm inside, because most of those are a gimmick. The best kinds are made from the *espadin* agave plant and produced around the region of Oaxaca.

MOLASSES This ingredient is used only as a way to substitute some of the flavor of the *piloncillo* if you can't find it. Avoid using the blackstrap kind because the flavor is too intense.

NATA This is the fat that rises to the top when raw milk is boiled to be pasteurized. It is very flavorful and rich and is used as a spread and an ingredient in some recipes. You can substitute it for clotted cream and it can be found in many high-end supermarkets, in ethnic grocery stores, or on the Internet.

NUTS There are many different nuts used in these recipes. The wonderful flavor from all of them comes from the oils, but it is also the reason why they often taste rancid. If you buy them from an open container, make sure you taste them first. Buy from a vacuum-sealed bag or a tightly sealed container if you can. Store them in a dry, cool area but refrigerate them or freeze them once they are opened so they last longer. Refrigerated nuts will last for about 3 months and frozen ones up to a year, but make sure they are tightly sealed as well as in a bag or a container. If you freeze them, thaw before using or bake for about 10 minutes in a 300°F oven.

PEPITAS The seeds from different types of squash and pumpkin are dried and used in many savory and sweet preparations. There are off-white to green ones and they vary in size. They can be found raw, roasted, salted, covered in chile, candied, hulled, or ground in markets all over Mexico. The pumpkin seeds used for these recipes are the hulled green, unroasted, unsalted ones found in many large grocery stores, health food stores, and ethnic markets. Store them in a tightly sealed bag or container in the fridge or freezer so the oil doesn't go rancid.

PILONCILLO Unrefined sugar with a molassy flavor molded into rounds or, more commonly, cones. It varies from shades of very pale gold to very dark brown. It is also known as *panela* or *panocha* and is quite hard. Some supermarkets in Mexico now sell chopped *piloncillo*, but please stay away from them because, although it may seem convenient, the flavor is not the same and

Cooking with Sugar

There are several recipes in the book that ask you to cook sugar to a certain stage. These stages refer to the way the sugar acts once it has cooled, and each stage is achieved at a specific temperature.

It is easier to use a thermometer (even though I never actually encountered anyone in Mexico using one), but there is the old-fashioned method of taking a little bit of the cooked sugar and putting it into ice-cold water to determine which stage it's at. The accuracy in the temperature is vital for the end result. An under-cooked confection, for example, won't set properly, and an over-cooked one will be too hard.

I hope that this chart helps you and you feel a little less intimidated to try these recipes if you haven't worked with sugar before. All you need is a little patience and care. Once the sugar and water are mixed as indicated in the recipe, be sure to wipe the sides of the pot clean with a brush to avoid crystallization.

After a little cooked sugar is dropped into ice water with a cooking spoon or spatula, look for the following characteristics for each stage.

Thread:
The sugar forms a thread when stretched between your index finger and thumb.
215°–230°F

Soft Ball:
You can form a soft ball that flattens when you press it down.
235°–240°F

Firm Ball:
You can form a firm ball, but it's still a bit pliable.
245°F

Hard Ball:
You can form a ball that can't be squished and is rigid.
250°–260°F

Soft Crack:
The sugar will separate into hard threads that are pliable.
265°–270°F

Hard Crack:
The sugar will separate into threads that are quite brittle.
295°–310°F

some even melt in a very odd way. The best way to cut it is with a serrated knife and a bit of patience. It is hard to cut at first, but it will go much more easily once you've broken off a few large pieces. Store in a tightly sealed bag or jar in a dry, cool place for a very long time. You can find it in many Latin groceries and ethnic markets. In many cases, brown sugar can be substituted.

QUESO COTIJA Similar to Parmesan, this is a dry grating, slightly acidic, salty cheese.

QUESO FRESCO (FRESH CHEESE) A crumbly cheese that is slightly acidic and a bit salty.

REQUESÓN A soft ricotta-like cheese. You can substitute it with whole ricotta or pot cheese in equal amounts. Make sure you drain any excess liquid if necessary.

SALT I have used table salt for the recipes in this book because it's the most common, but if you prefer to use the coarser kosher kind, double the amount.

SEEDS Avoid buying any seeds in large containers because they will go rancid more rapidly. Store them in a dry, cool area and freeze or refrigerate in a tightly sealed jar or bag if you aren't going to use them for awhile.

SUPERFINE SUGAR This is granulated sugar that has been finely ground. It is used in a few recipes that require the sugar to dissolve more rapidly, but you can use the granulated kind if you can't find superfine.

TAMARIND Fresh tamarind grows as a brown curved pod with a hard shell that encapsulates the tart, velvety flesh. The outer shell needs to be peeled for all the preparations, so look for somewhere the skin peels off easily and make sure the flesh is tender. You can also find many tamarind derivatives, from fresh purées to concentrates and nectars. For these recipes, buy the fresh pods or pulp as directed. You can find them in many Latin grocery stores and Asian markets, but note that the tamarind from Mexico is more acidic and less fragrant than most of the Asian varieties.

TEJOCOTES Small fruits similar to a crabapple but quite tart, *tejocotes* are used in many Christmas preparations. You can easily find them in syrup if you want to try them. The fresh ones are harder to come by outside Mexico, so look for them in the frozen section of Latin markets.

TEQUILA A spirit made from the agave plant in the town of Tequila, Jalisco; the best kind is made with blue agave. The white or silver tequila is the lightest, the *reposado* has been aged in wooden barrels from 2 to 11 months, and the *añejo* is the strongest one because it has been aged for at least a year.

TOMATILLOS Small green acidic round fruits, filled with tiny edible seeds, encapsulated by a papery husk; a distant relative of the tomato. The flavor changes drastically when it's cooked. Look for tomatillos that are bright green for a sweeter flavor and a husk that is closely attached to the fruit. Peel away the husk and rinse in water to remove the stickiness. Store them in a paper bag inside the fridge for up to 2 to 3 weeks.

VANILLA This is one of the ingredients indigenous to Mexico in the town of Papantla, Veracruz. The pod grows on a type of orchid and must be hand-pollinated, which is one of the reasons why it's quite expensive. Although it originated in Mexico, only a very small percentage of the ones found today are produced there; its flavor is sweet, creamy, and a bit spicy. Some of the best vanilla beans come from Madagascar and Tahiti. Look for plump pods and store them tightly wrapped in plastic in a dry area or in the refrigerator, but don't freeze them because you will lose some of the subtleties in the flavor and aroma. When using vanilla extract, buying a good quality one makes a big difference. Look for pure vanilla extract made from vanilla beans, around 35 percent alcohol and water. It's okay if it has sugar, but please don't get artificial or imitation vanilla flavoring.

VEGETABLE OIL Always use a neutral oil, such as safflower, sunflower, or corn.

VEGETABLE SHORTENING Yes, I know this fat belongs in the new kind of "enemy" fats, but it is widely used in Mexico. I've included it in some recipes and as a substitution to lard because the texture it gives is incredibly flaky and simply cannot be fully replaced by butter. It is always a good idea, however, to combine it with some butter because shortening doesn't have any flavor, so one will provide the texture and the other the yumminess. Please don't be afraid—a little bit won't kill you.

ZAPOTE NEGRO The *zapote* fruit is round and about the size of a small orange. It has a thin green skin and a black interior, which is where the name comes from. It is quite sweet, and although it is eaten on its own, it is mostly used to prepare a dessert made with orange juice. Look for ones that feel very soft because they will be the sweetest.

Tomatillos, Tejocotes, Zapote negro

EQUIPMENT GUIDE

FOR EACH PIECE OF EQUIPMENT, there are often so many different types and varieties that it can be hard to select your best option if you're buying something for the first time—or even know if you in fact have what you need.

You may have a lot of the equipment listed in your kitchen already, but I've included certain common items here because there may be some information in the explanation that you'll find useful and will give your baking a boost. There are also some items you may be less familiar with; I've included ways to substitute those in case you can't find them. This is by no means an exhaustive list, but rather the items I consider essential to know and understand.

BAKING SHEETS There are many different kinds of baking sheets, but I suggest you get the high-quality heavy-duty kind that are 11 by 17 inches with ½-inch edges. These bake more evenly, are more resilient, and last longer. Have at least three, and make sure they cool down before you wash them so they don't bend or create hot spots.

BENCH OR DOUGH SCRAPER These are very good for handling sticky doughs such as yeast-based ones. They are rectangular, have a metal or wooden handle, and are particularly useful for portioning and cutting dough, transferring ingredients, and cleaning up surfaces.

BLENDER It is very useful to have an electric blender. Although the standing one is much stronger, a handheld one will work for many of the recipes.

CAKE PANS The best kinds are made of tin-plated steel or medium-weight aluminum. Look for pans that are sturdy with straight sides. Avoid the flexible kind because they will change the texture of the cakes, and don't buy dark metal pans because they absorb much more heat, which can lead to overbrowning.

CAKE TESTER This is a very thin piece of metal with a loop to hold it and is used to test when a cake is done, but it can be replaced with a toothpick or a skewer.

CHURRERA This tool is used to form *churros*. It works in the way a cookie press does, giving it the distinctive long, ridged look. It's sold in different sizes and materials.

COMAL A heavy round or oval griddle used to cook tortillas; made from different materials such as clay or metal. A few recipes call for a *comal*, which can be replaced with a skillet, griddle pan, or a cast-iron pan.

CUTTERS A set of graduated metal circles that have straight or ridged edges.

ELECTRIC MIXER A standing heavy-duty one is best. I know they can be expensive, but if you like baking, you simply must get one. It will make your life much easier, and it's wonderful for bread making and freeing up your hands. Choose one with a 4½- to 6-quart capacity, and make sure you have the three basic attachments: whisk, paddle, and hook.

FLAN MOLD These are made from thin tin and have 3 main parts. An outer container to hold the water, a mold for the flan, a lid, and often some clips to hold them together; they are used on the stove or in the oven. I haven't used a flan mold in any of the recipes because they are hard to find and because most ramekins or cake pans will work just fine; if you have one, dry it very well or it will rust. If using ramekins, you'll need a larger pan to hold them.

FOOD PROCESSOR This is one of those things that may seem a bit pricy and perhaps unnecessary, but once you have one you'll wonder how you could've ever been without one. They are very useful for chopping and grinding nuts, preparing doughs, and making several of the candies in the book.

GRATER A box-style one is very helpful to have around.

ICE CREAM MACHINE There are many different ice cream machines out there in a wide array of prices. You don't need to spend a fortune, but look for one that has at least a 1½-quart capacity and make sure that the base is fully chilled before using.

KNIVES Generally speaking, you'll need three kinds for baking: a small paring knife with a 2- to 3-inch blade to split vanilla beans, cut small things, and even peel; a 10- to 12-inch chef's knife, which is the multitask knife; and a serrated knife. I like the long offset kind, which are particularly useful for cutting large fruits, chopping *piloncillo,* and cutting through cakes.

LIME SQUEEZER This is a very useful tool found in most, if not all, Mexican kitchens. The best ones are the metal kind that look a bit beat up, but you can also find some good-quality ones made from acrylic. Buy a larger one so you can use it for lemons as well.

MEASURING CUPS AND SPOONS There's a reason why there are dry and liquid measuring cups, and it isn't to get you to buy more things but to have accuracy. You'll need liquid measuring cups, preferably a 1-cup and a 1-quart one (make sure you measure at eye level); a set of metal measuring cups ranging from ¼ cup to 1 cup; and a set of metal spoons that measure from ¼ teaspoon to 1 tablespoon. For the dry measuring cups and the measuring spoons, use the "dip and sweep method," dipping it into the ingredient and leveling it off with a knife.

METATE A rectangular piece of stone (most often volcanic rock) with three legs, slightly inclined, used to grind spices, corn, chiles, and cacao. This is not something I suggest you go out and buy because it is quite time-consuming to use, but it is important to note that it has been an essential tool used from pre-Hispanic times to this day, mainly in small towns and villages.

MIXING BOWLS The best and most useful are the stainless steel or Pyrex ones. Get a few in various sizes with tall sides. Don't get the stainless steel ones with the rubber bottoms, because you can't use them in a double boiler and you can always use a towel underneath to hold it steady.

MOLCAJETE AND TEJOLOTE These are essentially the mortar and pestle of Mexico made from volcanic rock and used to grind many spices and make salsas, but you can replace them with a spice grinder.

MOLINILLO A wooden hand-carved tool used as a sort of whisk; you turn it with the palms of your hands to froth Mexican hot chocolate. Look for *molinillos* that have several rings to make the foamiest froths.

MOLINO DE MANO A hand grinder used to grind small quantities of corn or spices; can be replaced by a food processor or spice/coffee grinder.

NONSTICK MAT Commonly referred to as Silpat, a brand name (and a great one); there are many others of very good quality. These flexible mats can be reused up to two thousand times. They may seem a bit pricy, but they save you a lot of paper and money in the long run, as long as you take good care of them. Rinse them with hot water and a sponge and lay them flat once they dry to store them. Never, ever fold them because they will tear in time.

OLLAS DE BARRO Earthenware pot commonly used for punch, hot chocolate, and coffee. The material gives it a very distinctive flavor. I've read warnings that the glaze has a high lead content, but I've basically ignored them because they have been used for a very long time in Mexico without any known repercussions. If you buy one, you will need to cure it before using it. Mix a bit of calcium oxide with water to form a paste, rub the paste all over the outside of the pot, and let it dry in the sun. Rinse, and that's it. Do not store anything inside it.

OVEN Success is dependent on accuracy, and in baking recipes, the oven is probably the most important tool. Test the accuracy of the temperature with an oven thermometer and reduce the temperature indicated by 25 degrees if you have a convection oven.

PALA DE MADERA Wooden spoons, particularly ones with a straight edge, are very useful in recipes that require a lot of stirring because they don't conduct heat. Keep some wooden spoons separate from the ones used for savory dishes, because they will absorb odors and flavors with time and you definitely don't want your caramel ice cream to taste like onion.

PARCHMENT PAPER This provides a great nonstick surface and is sold in sheets or rolls. You will find it very useful.

PASTRY BAGS These are made of polyester, nylon, and disposable plastic. Use whichever material you like, but make sure that you rinse and dry the polyester or nylon ones before you store them so they don't get moldy, and don't accidentally throw away the tip if you use the disposable plastic ones.

PASTRY BRUSH A small, flat brush 1 to 2 inches wide is best for the recipes in this book. You can buy one at a cooking supply or hardware store.

PASTRY TIPS You'll need a star tip for *churros* and a flat tip for a few of the other recipes, but don't get the very tiny ones.

POTS OR SAUCEPANS You will need at least a 2-quart and a 4-quart or 5-quart pot. Make sure they are deep, with straight sides, and heavy, particularly for the candy recipes. Unless specified in the recipe, use nonreactive ones made from materials such as stainless steel, enameled ceramic, or lined copper (unlined copper will react with a lot of foods, changing the color and flavor in a negative way).

ROLLING PIN I like the French cylinder kind, which is about 16 by 2 inches and has no handles, because I find that it is easier to roll out dough more evenly. This will work for all the recipes where you'll need a rolling pin, except for the *campechanas* (look in the recipe's headnote).

RULER A ruler is used to ensure accuracy in the specified recipes.

SCALE Although the recipes are written in volume measurements, there are times when you will need to weigh some items, such as butter, because some brands don't mark the measurements. Look for a small digital one that has ounces and grams.

SPATULAS You need at least two basic ones. A heat-resistant rubber spatula is very useful for stirring things that cook for a long time, and it has the flexibility to help fold and scrape batters. An offset metal spatula is extremely useful for spreading things evenly.

SPICE/COFFEE GRINDER This is a very inexpensive and useful tool to grind small quantities of spices. I can assure you that once you make freshly ground cinnamon you'll never use store bought again.

STRAINERS, SIFTERS, AND SIEVES Sifting ingredients helps aerate them and ensures there are no hard or dirty bits. There are different kinds of sifters, but I really like the *tamis* or drum-style sifter because the round shape and flat strainer make it easy to use for dry ingredients. A regular colander with a sturdy handle will work to strain most liquids, but when a recipe calls for a fine-mesh strainer, use a cone-shaped one with tiny holes that allows only liquid to go through. You can help the liquid pass through by tapping the side at a bit of an angle with the palm of your hand or gently using a small ladle to press down.

THERMOMETERS The first thermometer you'll need is a candy or frying thermometer that has a clip and can register temperatures up to 500°F; the other is an oven thermometer to make sure the temperature in your oven is accurate.

TIMER This is a useful tool, particularly if you're easily distracted, like I am. Many ovens, microwaves, watches, and even phones have timers built into them, so you may not need to purchase one. It's a good tool, but I see it as a backup. Rely on your other senses and trust your instincts.

TORTILLA PRESS This tool is used mostly in savory preparations, but there are a couple of recipes that call for one (you can always use your hand or a rolling pin between two pieces of plastic). Look for 6-inch ones that are metal or wood. Look at them at eye level to make sure there's an even space all around.

WHISK There are so many different kinds. The ones shaped like a balloon are good to incorporate a lot of air when whipping egg whites or cream, and most others are good for incorporating ingredients without adding much air. If you're only going to get one whisk, though, I suggest a 10- to 12-inch stainless steel sauce whisk.

WIRE RACK This simple tool allows air to circulate, which helps cookies or cakes cool evenly. It is also handy for allowing excess sauce or icing to drip, as in the *frusta cristalizadas*.

ZESTER I suggest the microplane kind with a handle (these tend to last longer) because I find it to be the most efficient for zesting citrus and shaving small amounts of hard cheese and chocolate.

BEBIDAS

—

BEVERAGES

PERHAPS MEXICO'S MOST FAMOUS BEVERAGE around the globe is tequila, but that represents only a fraction of the wonderful drinks found throughout the country. The first beverage known in Mexico was the *octli*, or *pulque*, but others such as *balche*; corn-based drinks like *nahua*, *chichi*, and *izquiate*; and fermented fruit drinks date back to pre-Hispanic times as well.

Carl Lumholtz talks about the common corn beverages in his book *Unknown Mexico*. He writes, "Nothing is closer to the heart of the Tarahumaras as the liquor called *tesgüiño*. It looks like milky water and the taste is not very appealing. To make it, maize is soaked then cooked and ground, adding a seed that resembles wheat so it ferments. It is poured into specially made ceramic vats, where it is left for at least 24 hours." This beverage was very important for the Tarahumaras, who used it ceremoniously. They gave it to children with their mothers' breast milk, as medicine; it was "sprinkled" on newborns by the *curandero* (traditional folk healer); and women would drink it when going to seek a husband.

Historically in Mexico, beverages, alcoholic and nonalcoholic, particularly the homemade, have always been used as part of rituals, during religious festivities, and for medicinal purposes. The list of regional uses is endless. An example is the Selva Lacandona's ceremonial *balche*, which is sweetened with the honey of a specific bee (its honey is used solely for this purpose) and must be consumed the day it is made.

There are many similar beverages that can be found throughout Mexico, but their preparation or name will vary depending on where they are made; these include *atoles*, *aguardientes*, *rompope*, *pulques*, and hot chocolate. Many times the name of a beverage is given by the person who made that particular combination or the name alludes to the main flavor, particularly in those with indigenous roots and made in small batches.

Nowadays, there are more than sixty ethnic communities in Mexico. Each community has its own festivities, and each town or *mayordomía* has its own celebrations of the patron saints. Each year a member of the community is chosen as the *mayordomo* and is in charge of the festivity and, of course, the wide selection of beverages, because it wouldn't be a celebration without them.

The sugarcane *aguardiente* is associated with Colonial times and was consumed mainly by the people who worked on the sugarcane plantations. The Spanish drank wine, and the Indians had their *pulque*.

The conquerors brought wine and sugarcane, together with new fruits. Later on, the *alambique* arrived via a distillation process of Arab origin; with newfound fruits, other beverages were transformed and new ones emerged.

Beverages definitely play an important role in the sweet culture of Mexico, and the country offers an unparalleled selection: refreshing and colorful *aguas frescas* (popular drinks made with fresh fruit or seeds, water, and sugar); the wonderfully rich, corn-thickened chocolate beverage, *champurrado*, a usual partner to sweet tamales; the *aguamiel* from the maguey plant spiced with a bit of chile in Hidalgo; *achocote*, a corn beverage sweetened with *piloncillo*; *crema de coco*, a luscious, nonalcoholic coconut beverage made from fresh coconut and milk in Colima; the sweet *toritos* from Veracruz, made with peanuts, *guanábana* (soursop), or *jobo* (a velvety yellow plum) mixed with condensed milk and enjoyed at the end of a meal; and the wonderfully frothy hot chocolate from Oaxaca for dipping *pan dulce*.

3 ½ cups whole milk or water

6 to 8 Chocolate Tablets (recipe follows), broken into pieces

Theobroma cacao, the botanical name meaning "food from the gods," captures the magnificent essence of the cacao bean. It's the perfect way to start the journey through the sweets of Mexico because it is also considered one of the most important contributions from the land to the world. Cacao was consumed by the Olmecas as early as 1500 B.C.E. Mayan priests used it for religious rituals, mixing it with chiles, vanilla, and honey. The Mexica indians consumed it hot or cold and mixed it with ground corn, vanilla (the orchid and the bean), magnolia flowers, *achiote*, allspice, or honey, and used the bean as currency. It was (and continues to be) energetically beaten with a *molinillo*, poured from up high so it is foamy, and often taken in ceramic cups or *jícaras* (gourd bowls).

In Mesoamerica, the fruit of the cacao symbolized the human heart, and the ground toasted bean symbolized the blood. Moctezuma Xocoyotzin offered the first chocolate beverage to Hernán Cortés. Cortés sent cacao to Europe as a tribute to Spain, explaining the different uses and the importance it had in Tenochtitlan; it quickly became the preferred beverage of the king. In Mexico, chocolate remains an ingredient used primarily in beverages.

Its importance has lasted many centuries, and there are many different kinds of chocolate mixtures. Many places preserve the tradition of slowly toasting the beans on a *comal*, peeling them (an *atole* is sometimes made from the shells), and grinding them by hand over a warm *molinillo*; others go to a community mill. Either way, most mix it with

CONTINUED

Addiction to Chocolate

The addiction to chocolate has created a lot of conflict and even some deaths. Don Artemio de Valle-Arizpe wrote a story about Bernardino de Salazar y Frías, a bishop from Chiapas who forbid excess consumption in 1625. Distinguished society ladies would drink chocolate at all hours of the day, even in church—their maids would bring the foamy hot beverage to them as they sat in the pews. Apparently they were very unhappy about the new restrictions: they say the bishop died from a poisoned cup of hot chocolate. It is still customary to say in Chiapas, "They gave him his chocolate," when someone is murdered.

sugar and cinnamon (the cinnamon is also toasted and ground, in most cases). Then tablets or balls are formed from this granular mixture and left to dry in the shade. The ones with almonds, vanilla, and/or spices are usually reserved for special occasions.

I wanted to make my own in a modern kitchen using a food processor because much of the hot chocolate that is exported doesn't have almonds and uses artificial flavoring (luckily, though, a couple of really good brands are becoming more available); I was very happy with the results. You can make the hot chocolate with water or milk and use a whisk if you don't have a *molinillo*, but make sure it is really frothy and hot when you drink it.

In a saucepot over medium heat, bring the milk to a boil, add the chocolate tablets (the quantity depends on how strong you like hot chocolate), and decrease the heat, stirring until the chocolate is dissolved. Froth with a *molinillo*, whisk, or hand mixer until you have a nice bubbly foam and serve immediately.

MAKES ABOUT 1 QUART

CHOCOLATE TABLETS

Preheat the oven to 350°F.

Place the almonds and *canela* on separate baking sheets and roast, turning often, until everything is toasted; the *canela* should take about 5 minutes and the almonds 10 minutes (remove the *canela* while the almonds continue to toast). Remove from the oven and let cool on a plate. (You could do this on the stove instead using a *comal* or griddle over moderate heat but you'll need to pay close attention to it.)

Lay the cacao beans in a single layer on another baking sheet. Once the almonds are done, put the cacao beans in the oven and decrease the heat to 300°F (the initial hotter temperature will give the almonds a nice roasted flavor). Make sure you move the beans around often so they roast evenly, and bake until they all change color and the outer shells begin to crack slightly, 15 to 20 minutes. The best test, however, is to smell them. Make sure you don't overroast the beans or they will be bitter.

Remove the beans from the oven and let cool slightly so they are easier to handle. Remove the outer shells with your hands by pressing

1 cup whole almonds

5 (3-inch) pieces of *canela*

1 pound cacao beans

3 to 3 ½ cups sugar

each bean lightly. Try a bean; it should have a nice roasted flavor and shouldn't be bitter, but may be acidic because of the tannins.

Grind the cooled beans in a food processor for awhile until they are all "melted" into a smooth paste (you'll know what I mean when you get there; just be patient), scraping down the sides as needed.

Coarsely chop the almonds, break the *canela* into small pieces, and add to the cacao, continuing to grind. Add the sugar, starting with 3 cups and add a little more, if needed, depending on the beans (the mixture should be sweet but not overly so). Continue grinding for awhile longer until everything comes together. The mixture should be smooth and slightly grainy.

Line an 11 by 17-inch baking sheet with a nonstick mat or wax paper, pour the chocolate mixture onto it, and flatten with your hands or a spatula (use a little cold water in either case so it doesn't stick). Make sure it is spread out evenly. Using a sharp knife, lightly mark the tablets to your desired size (I like to do 1 inch by 2 inches) with a ruler, dipping the knife in a container of hot water and drying it as needed so it doesn't stick. Allow them to fully set (usually overnight), then separate the tablets and store in an airtight container in a dry place. They should last about 3 months if stored properly. They may discolor with time, but this doesn't mean they are spoiled.

MAKES 2½ TO 3 POUNDS

Chocolate de metate
(chocolate tablets)

5 cups water

3 ounces *piloncillo*, coarsely chopped, or ⅓ cup firmly packed dark brown sugar

½ cup sugar

1 cup fresh masa, or 1 cup masa harina mixed with ½ cup hot water

1½ cups fresh blackberries

The word *atole* comes from *atl,* "water," and *tlaoli,* "ground corn." These beverages have been consumed since pre-Hispanic times and the variations are countless. Made with water, milk, or a combination of the two, and commonly thickened with masa, the beverage is also made with ground toasted corn, fermented corn, rice, oatmeal, fresh corn, or mature corn cooked in ashes. It is sweetened with sugar and/or *piloncillo* and often mixed with fruit.

This drink is enjoyed with sweet tamales early in the morning or at night. This *atole* is very popular in Michoacán, and I want to thank Ernesto Hernandez Doblas for the recipe.

In a saucepot over high heat, bring the water to a boil with the *piloncillo* and sugar until they are dissolved. Add the masa and whisk so it dissolves and doesn't form any lumps. Let thicken.

Purée the blackberries in a food processor, add to the mixture, and cook for a couple of minutes; do not boil too long or the drink will lose color and that fresh blackberry flavor. Enjoy it while it's warm. If you have any left over it will thicken quite a bit; you can store it in the refrigerator and simply add a bit of water to the mixture when you reheat it.

MAKES ABOUT 1½ QUARTS

VARIATION: STRAWBERRY ATOLE

2½ cups water

2½ cups whole milk

¾ to 1 cup sugar

1 cup fresh masa, or 1 cup masa harina mixed with ½ cup hot water

2 pints fresh strawberries

Prepare as with the blackberry *atole*, combining the water, milk, and sugar (the quantity will depend on how sweet your strawberries are). Add the masa as directed. Purée the strawberries and combine in the same manner. Serve warm.

Atole de Amaranto | Amaranth Porridge

Amaranth was a primary source of protein and an essential part of the diet for the pre-Hispanic population of Mesoamerica. It was often described as the "golden grain of the gods."

The seeds from the plant are considered one of the most nutritious grains and are a good substitute for wheat for those on a gluten-free diet. I like it simply for the flavor. I think it's pretty awesome that the conquistadors forbade its cultivation because it was associated with human sacrifice, and yet, because of some "rebels" who valued the importance of their culture and traditions, it is still around thousands of years later. That surely should not go unnoticed!

You can buy amaranth flour and puffed amaranth in some health or specialty food shops and online (see Sources).

3 cups water

1 (3-inch) piece *canela*

1½ cups amaranth flour

⅓ cup honey

½ cup puffed amaranth

Place the water and *canela* in a pot over medium heat and bring to a boil. Slowly whisk in the amaranth flour so it doesn't form lumps. Decrease the heat to low. Cook, stirring frequently, until the mixture has thickened and starts to boil again. Stir in the honey, remove from the heat, discard the *canela*, and pour into serving bowls. Top each bowl with some puffed amaranth and serve warm.

SERVES 4

Fray Bernardino Sahagún, a Spanish missionary of the Franciscan order and author of the seminal *Florentine Codex: General Book of Things of The New Spain,* wrote in 1565 that indigenous peoples sold hot and cold *atoles* made from ground or toasted corn that ancient Mexicans called *atolli*.

12 ounces dried white corn kernels (don't use the kind for popcorn)

1 (3-inch) piece *canela*

6 ounces *piloncillo*, finely chopped, or ¾ cup firmly packed dark brown sugar

This is a wonderful beverage made from toasted ground corn sweetened with sugar or *piloncillo*. You can find it prepared, already ground and ready to be mixed with water or milk. Additional flavors vary depending on the region and include anise, oatmeal, allspice, chocolate, and cinnamon, the most common. It is a very tasty, refreshing, and energizing drink, especially when served cold.

Rinse the corn kernels under cold water and drain. Dry completely with a towel, and then toast in a skillet or *comal* over medium heat, stirring frequently, until they have changed color and smell a bit nutty but not burned. Once they are cool, grind in a food processor together with the *canela* and *piloncillo* (you can also leave out the sweetener and add it later when you make the drink). Store in an airtight container in a dry, cool area and simply mix with water or milk when desired, using 4 to 6 tablespoons of *pinole* per 1 cup liquid.

MAKES 3 TO 4 CUPS

Ponteduro

Ponteduro is the name of a sweet, crumbly candy made from *pinole* and honey and cut into squares.

Rompope | Eggnoglike Beverage

It is believed that in the eighteenth century, egg whites were used as a sort of glue to bind sheets of golden and white gold. There were many leftover yolks that were then used to create various sweets and to thicken others, such as *rompope*. This eggnoglike beverage is wonderful served cold year-round. I like to put it in the *tres leches* mixture (page 142), use it to top ice cream, and make a gelatin with it (page 138). It is still sold in many convents around Mexico. Estela Romo de Vivar makes one of the tastiest almond versions I've had.

Combine the milk, sugar, baking soda, and *canela* in a large pot and bring to a boil over medium-high heat. Decrease the heat and cook for 30 minutes at a soft boil; it will reduce to about 3 cups. In a heatproof bowl, whisk the egg yolks lightly by hand and slowly pour in about 1 cup of the hot milk mixture, whisking continuously. Return the mixture to the pot and cook over low heat, stirring often until the mixture has thickened slightly and resembles the consistency of half-and-half, 5 to 7 minutes. Remove from the heat and immediately pour into a bowl placed in an ice bath to chill. Discard the *canela* and gently whisk in the rum and vanilla. Chill completely before serving.

MAKES ABOUT 5 CUPS

1 quart whole milk

1 cup sugar

Pinch of baking soda

1 (3-inch) piece *canela*

8 egg yolks

½ cup dark rum or brandy

1 teaspoon pure vanilla extract (optional)

VARIATION: ALMOND ROMPOPE

Put the almonds in a small pot and cover with cold water. Place over medium heat and bring to a boil. Turn off the heat and let sit for 2 minutes. Drain and reserve until cool enough to handle. Remove the skins by pressing the almonds lightly (they should come off easily) and discard the skins. Dry any excess moisture with a paper towel and finely grind in a food processor or coffee grinder.

Prepare the *rompope* as above, combining the milk, baking soda, and nutmeg, but take about 1 cup of the warm milk once it has reduced and cool slightly over ice. Add the almonds to the 1 cup milk, and purée in an electric blender (it will be slightly grainy). Reserve. Whisk the yolks as directed above and add to the pot, then add the almond mixture. Discard the nutmeg and gently whisk in the orange liqueur. Chill completely before serving.

⅔ cup whole almonds, unpeeled

1 quart whole milk

Pinch of baking soda

1 small (½-inch) piece fresh nutmeg

6 egg yolks

½ cup orange liqueur

Café de Olla | Aromatic Sweet Coffee

6 cups water

1 large (6-inch) piece *canela*, broken into 2 or 3 pieces

2 whole cloves

3 ounces *piloncillo*, chopped, or ⅓ cup firmly packed dark brown sugar plus 1 teaspoon molasses

1 strip orange zest, no pith (optional)

6 tablespoons freshly ground dark roast coffee

Before roasters existed, coffee used to be toasted in ceramic plates and ground in hand mills or *metates* (a stone tool used to grind seeds and other ingredients) in small batches. Many small towns still prefer to hand grind their beans to prepare this aromatic spiced coffee.

Combine the water, *canela*, cloves, *piloncillo*, and zest in a clay pot or stainless steel pot and cook over medium heat until the *piloncillo* dissolves. Simmer for 5 minutes, then add the ground coffee. Stir and continue to simmer for 5 minutes more without allowing it to come to a boil. Strain and serve.

MAKES 6½ TO 7 CUPS

Ponche Navideño | Christmas Fruit Punch

2 quarts water

2 (6-inch) pieces *canela*, cut into pieces

8 ounces *tejocotes*, left whole

6 large guavas, peeled and cut into large bite-size pieces

2 Gala, Fuji, or Golden Delicious apples, peeled, cored, and cut into large bite-size pieces

2 (4-inch) pieces sugarcane, peeled and cut into pieces

1 cup pitted prunes, halved lengthwise

½ cup dark raisins

5 long tamarind pods, peeled and seeded, or 3 tablespoons tamarind pulp (no seeds)

6 to 8 ounces chopped *piloncillo* or dark brown sugar

¾ cup rum, brandy, or tequila (optional)

This is a very fragrant fruit punch enjoyed in the *posada*s and at end-of-year reunions all over Mexico. It is cooked in large batches and the aroma warms you from the moment it reaches your nose. Adults enjoy the punch with a bit of booze and call it *piquete*. I particularly like the ones made with tamarind because of the nice tartness that balances the sweetness of the *piloncillo*. Hibiscus flowers can be used if you want a nice burgundy color. Feel free to replace the fruits that you can't find or don't like for those of your own choosing.

Combine the water, *canela*, and *tejocotes* in a large pot and bring to a boil over high heat. Decrease the heat to maintain a constant soft simmer and cook for about 5 minutes, or until the *tejocotes* are soft. Remove from the heat, scoop out the *tejocotes*, then peel them and remove the hard bit. Return them to the pot and add the guavas, apples, sugarcane, prunes, raisins, tamarind, and *piloncillo*. Simmer for at least 30 minutes, stirring gently. Add the liquor, discard the *canela*, pour into cups, and serve.

MAKES 3 QUARTS

Champurrado | Chocolate-Corn Porridge

This is one of the oldest beverages in Mexico and uses two of the main ingredients indigenous to the Americas: cacao and corn. It is essentially a thick corn beverage made with a bit of chocolate and lightly sweetened. It is sold in markets, outside bus stations, and near churches. It is present at many celebrations, from birthdays to baptisms, and is a popular accompaniment to sweet tamales.

This recipe was given to me in the state of Tabasco, where I visited some wonderful cacao plantations that are lucky enough to have the ivory *criollo* bean, one of the highest quality in the world. Originally, *champurrado* was made with the shells of the toasted beans, but it is now made with the chocolate tablets used for *chocolate caliente*. If you don't have any homemade tablets or can't find them in the store, you can substitute the same amount of bittersweet chocolate and add another stick of *canela*.

Combine the fresh masa with the 1½ cups water and the *canela* in a medium pot and cook over medium heat, stirring with a whisk, until it begins to bubble. Add the milk, chocolate, and *piloncillo*. Bring the mixture to a simmer, stirring until everything is melted and blended together. Discard the *canela*. Serve as is or strain it if desired (the slightly grainy texture is more authentic, however, and I actually quite like it).

MAKES 1 QUART

½ cup fresh masa, or
½ cup masa harina mixed
with ⅓ cup hot water

1½ cups water

1 (3-inch) piece *canela*

3 cups whole milk

3 ounces Chocolate Tablets
(page 26)

2 ounces chopped *piloncillo*,
or ⅓ cup raw sugar and
2 teaspoons molasses

Pozol

Pozol is another wonderful beverage that has been around since pre-Hispanic times; it is made with toasted corn and water, left to ferment in some regions, and then served ice cold.

3 dried vanilla beans, split lengthwise

1½ cups sugar

1½ cups water

2½ cups rum or vodka

Although the name of this drink in Spanish translates into "vanilla oil," this is no such thing. You can use fresh whole vanilla beans, but this recipe is a good way to use up ones you've stored from other recipes. It is a very subtle and lovely drink that I enjoyed in Veracruz, where the beautiful orchid first appeared.

Chop the vanilla beans into small pieces or leave them whole. Combine the sugar and water in a pot over medium heat, stirring until the sugar dissolves, and then add the vanilla beans. Pour into a large container, stir, add the rum, and cover tightly. Store in a dry, dark place for 4 to 7 days (you can try it after 4 days to see how you like it and leave it longer if it needs a bit more flavor). Strain through a fine-mesh sieve or cheesecloth if desired or leave as is and store in a sterilized jar. Serve chilled. This will keep for about 2 months in a cool, dry place.

MAKES 1 QUART

Pasita | Raisin Liqueur

In the antiques shop area Los Sapos, in the state of Puebla, there's a charming little bar named for this drink, which is their specialty. The scene is a continuous movement of people enjoying the shot glasses of this raisin liqueur served with a toothpick studded with a cube of salty cheese and a raisin. Their recipe is secret, but this is very close to it.

1½ cups sugar

1 cup water

3 cups brandy

2 cups dark raisins

Combine the sugar and water in a pot over medium heat, and cook, stirring, until the sugar dissolves. Pour into a large container. Stir in about 1 cup of the brandy, add the raisins, and let macerate until the raisins are plump, about 20 minutes. Add the remaining 2 cups brandy and cover tightly. Store in a dry, dark place for 2 weeks. Strain through a fine-mesh sieve or cheesecloth and store in a sterilized jar. Although this drink is typically served at room temperature, I like it a bit chilled. It will keep for about 2 months in the refrigerator.

MAKES ABOUT 5 CUPS

Ratafia de Durazno | Peach Liqueur

Ratafias are cordials made from macerated infused fruits, herbs, flowers, or spices; they make a wonderful digestif. Be sure to keep in a dry place away from direct sunlight while the liqueur steeps.

1½ cups sugar, or 1 cup honey

¾ cup water

2 pounds ripe peaches

1 quart brandy, rum, or vodka

Combine the sugar and water in a pot over medium heat, stirring until the sugar dissolves. Remove from the heat and let cool.

Slice the peaches in half lengthwise to remove the pit and put these inside a cloth. Carefully but firmly crack them open with the bottom of a heavy pot or a hammer to remove the almond inside; discard the outer part.

Coarsely chop the peaches and combine in a large jar with the sugar syrup, peach almonds, and brandy. Cover tightly, store in a dry, dark place, and stir or shake every 4 or 5 days. Try it after 3 weeks and continue doing so until enough flavor has been extracted (but steep for no longer than 5 weeks).

Strain once and press down lightly on the solids. Strain again through a cheesecloth and repeat if there are any small pieces left. Store in a sterilized jar and refrigerate. It will keep for about 1 month.

MAKES ABOUT 5 CUPS

DULCES DE CONVENTO

—

SWEETS FROM THE CONVENTS

THE SKILL OF NUNS IN THE KITCHEN is very well known, but it is their devotion, religious purpose, and patience that gave birth to many of the wonderful sweets of Mexico. In *History of the Gastronomy in Mexico City*, Salvador Novo wrote, "And when sugar arrived [in] this land, the fruits of this were absorbed through the delicate hands of the nuns." He goes on to describe a miraculous crystal liquid made from sugar and water that embraced a wide array of fruits and lists a number of sweet preparations that are still made to this day, including *cabello de angel*, fruit pastes, and various fruits in syrup.

The births of many adored sweets are, in fact, attributable to the nuns' diligent hands, particularly those from Andalucía, who had a strong African influence. This era of *mestizaje* blended religion, knowledge, and tradition and led to a newfound vibrancy in the culinary arts.

The first convent of New Spain was founded in 1530 and named the Real Convento de la Concepción. Many others would soon follow. Even though they may have had vegetable gardens or stables, convents in general needed additional income. Many received it through teaching young girls from wealthy families, training them in catechism and teaching them how to set a table, sew, play an instrument, and bake. Others sold culinary creations and would often lure potential donors with elaborate and delicious sweets.

Despite the many rules of the convents, the nuns found a way to escape the rigors of religious life by concocting new flavors in the kitchen. With delicate, slow sweetness, they stirred and crafted, faithfully kneaded, and daringly named their sweets *beso* (kiss), *bien me sabe* (tastes so good to me), and *suspiro* (sigh).

When the Spaniards arrived, the Aztec *tecuilli* (three stones that enclosed the fireplace) were replaced by the cavelike *calabazero*, wood-fired ovens, and the mestizo kitchen was brought to new culinary heights. The tools in the kitchen from the old and the New Spain coexisted happily, surrounded by colorful *talavera* tile. Copper and ceramic pots adorned the wall next to sieves, mortars and pestles grinded next to *metates*, new spices seasoned the mestizo kitchen, and the handcrafted *cantaros* (jars) held water and oils.

European recipes, particularly those of Mediterranean and Arabic origin, were made by Spanish women, who were soon cooking together with mestizo, Creole, Filipino, and black women. The slaves from the Caribbean and Africa added their flavorings, and all these influences contributed to the wonderful sweets from the Viceroyalty era. The nuns made gifts that

were for the viceroys, archbishops, ecclesiastic dignitaries, and Mother Superiors (and I am pretty sure they saved some for themselves).

Some convents forbade or rationed chocolate; others prepared it but only as a beverage. It wasn't until the beginning of the nineteenth century that it was used in other preparations. Legend has it that Sor Juana Inés de la Cruz—a very important writer who became a nun because she wanted the freedom to embrace her intellect without dealing with all the responsibilities and requirements of a married woman, not because of her devotion to God—used to send little sweet messages of chocolate or confections with some kind of note hidden inside an embroidered shoe to intellectuals and poets.

Each order specialized in different things. The Franciscans made caramelized *yemitas*, syrup-coated *aleluyas de piñón*, and elaborate *alfeñiques* in the shapes of doves, lions, dogs, and sheep for the nativity scene; the Clarisas made *ladrillos de mamón* (a type of sliced pound cake soaked in syrup and rice pudding with ornate cinnamon symbols and pine nuts); the virgins of Santa Catalina poured *cajeta* (goat's milk caramel) into boxes made from the orange tree, infusing it with the wonderful scent of orange blossoms; and the Bernardinas specialized in fruit preparations such as *tejocote* jellies that were poured into molds in the shapes of flowers and hearts. There are convents that still prepare some of these sweets, but the ones in Puebla are particularly renowned.

Perhaps the most famous patron of the kitchen is San Pascual Bailón, a sixteenth-century shepherd who later joined the monastery. Although he was a lay brother in the kitchen, it is said that prayers would often consume him, causing him to neglect his responsibilities in the kitchen—which he was never actually fond of. The other Franciscans believed that he was elevated by angels, who would cook for him, leading them to say that his dishes were almost angelic. There are many illustrations, paintings, and carvings of this "patron of cooks," whose first appearance was in the convents. A lesser-known pastry patron, San Diego de Alcala, was called on often to help the nuns resist the temptations of the sweetness in the air.

1 cup whole almonds, skins on

1 cup sugar, plus extra for topping

¼ cup water

7 ounces (scant ½ cup) unsalted butter, softened

5 egg yolks

¼ teaspoon salt

2¼ cups all-purpose flour, sifted

2 egg whites

Sliced or slivered almonds, for topping

These cookies are unusual because you must make caramelized almonds, grind them, and then add them to the dough. But it's worth it because it gives them a lovely and unexpected crunch.

Preheat the oven to 350°F.

Place the almonds on a baking sheet and toast until golden in the center, 8 to 10 minutes. Remove from the oven and let cool completely.

Place a nonstick mat on a baking sheet or lightly grease the pan. Combine the 1 cup sugar and the water in a small saucepan, wiping the edges with a wet brush or your wet hands so no crystals form, and cook until it turns a golden caramel color. Add the almonds and stir quickly with a heatproof spatula or wooden spoon. Pour onto the prepared baking sheet. Let cool, and then grind in a food processor until the consistency resembles little sugar rocks but not powder.

Cream the butter in a mixer until pale and fluffy, and then add the egg yolks, one at a time. In a small bowl, combine the salt and flour and add gradually to the batter, scraping the sides as needed. Add the ground caramelized almonds until just combined.

Put about one-fourth of the mixture between two pieces of parchment paper (the size of your baking sheet) and roll out to about ¼-inch thickness. Keeping the rolled-out mixture between the parchment sheets, transfer to the baking sheet then place in the freezer for 10 minutes; repeat the process with the rest of the dough. Remove the baking sheets from the freezer, one at a time, beginning with the one that has been in the freezer the longest. Carefully peel off one of the parchment pieces to expose the cookie dough, and then put it back lightly, flip over the cookie dough, and peel off the other sheet. (This step makes the cookies easier to handle.)

Line a baking sheet with parchment paper. Cut out 2½-inch circles of dough (or whatever shape you desire) and place on the baking sheet. Repeat the process with the rest of the dough and gather the scraps to roll again. The scraps can be rerolled up to three times. If the dough starts to feel sticky, refrigerate or freeze it briefly.

Preheat the oven to 350°F.

Beat the egg whites lightly and brush the tops of the cookies. Decorate with sliced or slivered almonds and a bit of sugar. Bake until the edges begin to brown, about 10 minutes. Let cool for 5 minutes in the pan, and then transfer to a wire rack to cool completely.

MAKES 3 TO 4 DOZEN

Ciruelas Rellenas de Almendra | Almond-Stuffed Prunes

Almonds were used in most of the convents, and these prunes filled with an almond candy similar to marzipan capture the love the nuns had for this ingredient. You can always buy almond flour, but I find that the flavor of the nut really comes through when you make it at home, and the honey adds a delightful sweetness. You can fill dried figs, dried apricots, or dates instead.

TO MAKE THE ALMOND FLOUR, put the almonds in a small pot and cover with cold water. Bring to a boil over medium heat. Turn off the heat and let sit for 2 minutes. Drain and reserve until cool enough to handle. Remove the skins by pressing the almonds lightly (they should come off easily) and discard the skins. Dry any excess moisture with a paper towel and finely grind in a food processor or coffee grinder.

Combine the ½ cup sugar, 2 tablespoons of the honey, and the water in a pot and bring to a boil over medium heat. Add the ground almonds and stir continuously until starting to thicken. Stir in the vanilla and let cool. You can leave it like this or transfer to a food processor to get a smoother paste. Add the egg white and mix well. Add the remaining 2 tablespoons sugar and stir (this will give a slightly grainy and crunchy texture)

Slit open the prunes on one side and stuff them with a bit of the almond paste (slightly dampen your hands if it's too sticky and to smooth it). Heat the remaining 2 tablespoons honey in a small pan and brush over the tops of the prunes.

MAKES ABOUT 2 DOZEN

Almond flour

1½ cups whole almonds, skins on

½ cup plus 2 tablespoons sugar

4 tablespoons honey

3 tablespoons water

¼ teaspoon pure vanilla extract

1 egg white (optional)

24 prunes, pitted

Rosquetes Impregnados de Espiritu de Anís | Anise Cookies

This recipe is based on one in a magnificent book called *Delicias de antaño* by Teresa Castelló Yturbide and María Josefa Martínez del Río de Redo. The anise flavor comes from toasted aniseed as well as anise liqueur. These cookies are a unique preparation, because they are submerged in a sweet syrup after baking and dusted with sugar once they've dried out.

Sift the flour into a bowl. Melt the shortening in a small pan and add the aniseed. Heat for a couple of minutes over low-medium heat, making sure they don't burn, and then pour onto the flour. Mix with a spoon carefully but rapidly so no lumps are formed. Add the liqueur and lime zest.

Turn out onto a lightly floured surface and knead until a smooth and uniform dough is formed, 3 to 5 minutes. With your hands, roll out pieces about 5 inches wide and ½ inch thick, starting in the center and rolling outward so that the pieces are evenly thick. Connect one end of each piece to the other, making a ring, and place on a parchment-lined baking sheet, about 1 inch apart. Refrigerate until firm.

Preheat the oven to 350°F. Bake the cookies until slightly firm to the touch, about 10 minutes. Transfer to a wire rack to cool.

TO MAKE THE SYRUP, combine the water and sugar in a small pot over medium heat and cook until the sugar dissolves, 3 to 5 minutes. Remove from the heat and add the liqueur. Dip the tops of the cookies into the syrup and let dry on a rack. Pour any remaining syrup over the cookies and let cool completely.

Dust with the confectioner's sugar mixture and enjoy (they are best eaten the same day).

MAKES ABOUT 30

2 cups all-purpose flour

½ cup (4 ounces) vegetable shortening

1 teaspoon aniseed

1 tablespoon anise liqueur

Zest of 1 lime

Syrup

¼ cup water

½ cup sugar

1 teaspoon anise liqueur

Sifted confectioner's sugar mixed with a bit of freshly ground *canela*, for dusting

1 ½ cups unsalted butter

1 cup superfine sugar

2 cups all-purpose flour

1 cup almond flour

½ teaspoon pure vanilla extract

Sifted confectioner's sugar, for dusting

These cookies are fragile and it is almost impossible not to get crumbs all over the place when eating them, but that is precisely their beauty! The Arabs brought *polvorones* to Spain during their occupation, and the Spaniards, in turn, brought the cookies to Mexico when they settled in the land. The recipes differ in several ways, but the main difference is the Arabs used butter and the Spanish used lard. Nowadays, you can find both kinds in Mexico and others made with shortening or margarine. I tested many, many recipes, because I wanted the most crumbly, melt-in-your-mouth cookie with the least amount of human error possible. I ended up with this recipe, which is a hybrid of the two and may be made with or without nuts.

To clarify the butter, cut the butter into pieces and melt in a saucepan over low heat. Skim off any foam and discard. Turn off the heat and let sit for 5 minutes or so, until the remaining milk solids sink to the bottom. Gently strain the butter, making sure not to include the solids. Measure 1 cup.

Preheat the oven to 375°F.

In a bowl, combine the warm butter with the sugar and refrigerate until it solidifies, about 30 minutes. Remove from the refrigerator and whip until thickened (it'll look a bit like whipped cream). Stir in the all-purpose flour gradually, using a spoon or spatula, then add the almond flour and vanilla and combine. Knead, still in the bowl, with the palm of your hand until it starts to come together.

Turn out onto a lightly floured surface and roll out to about 1 inch thick, making sure the crumbly dough stays together. With a cookie cutter or glass, cut out 2-inch circles. They might crumble when you cut them as they are very fragile, so be gentle and patient, pressing the dough together as needed. Place on a baking sheet lined with a non-stick mat or parchment paper and bake until the edges are just starting to turn color (the tops should still be pale), 10 to 12 minutes. Let cool on the baking sheet for a few minutes. Dust them with confectioner's sugar and carefully transfer them from the baking sheet with an offset spatula; avoid touching them at all unless you are going to eat them.

MAKES ABOUT 2 DOZEN

NOTE: See page 42 to make your own almond flour; if you don't want to use nuts, you can substitute 1 cup flour.

1 pound unsalted pumpkin seeds

3½ cups sugar

1 cup water

½ teaspoon freshly ground *canela* (optional)

Red food coloring (optional)

Sifted confectioner's sugar, for rolling

Jamoncillo is the name of many different candies in Mexico, but they are usually firm on the outside and soft when you bite into them. Most commonly, you will see them in slices or blocks and made only from a couple of ingredients. This particular one is made from pumpkin seeds and sugar and is found primarily in central Mexico. The paste is often used to make a*lfeñiques*, or figures in various shapes. In Jalapa, Veracruz, you can still visit some convents where they make beautiful peach shapes that are molded around a square of wine-soaked cake.

Traditionally, this particular recipe was tinted using *grana cochinilla*, a small insect that comes from a cactus plant and is used to this day for its incredible vibrant red color. I've substituted it in this recipe with food coloring, but you can always leave it out. This preparation is a bit time-consuming because you have to soak the pumpkin seeds overnight and peel them, but the result is well worth the effort.

Soak the pumpkin seeds in abundant water overnight. Drain the water and peel the seeds, one by one, so that you only have the white part of the seed; discard the rest. (It's best if you can get some friends or family to help you with this part.)

Grind the seeds in a food processor or hand mill. If you have a hard time, add a bit of water, a little at a time, but no more than ¾ cup, until you have a fine paste.

Combine the sugar and water in a heavy-bottomed pot and cook over medium heat until you reach the thread stage (see page 13). Add the pumpkin seed paste and continue to cook over medium heat, stirring continuously with a wooden spoon or a heatproof spatula, until thickened. Remove from the heat and stir in the *canela*.

Line an 8 by 8-inch baking pan with parchment paper. Divide the mixture into three batches and tint one with enough food coloring to make it dark pink (almost fuchsia). Lightly dust a flat surface with a little confectioner's sugar and roll out the two uncolored batches, until they are about 1 inch thick. Roll out the dark pink batch the same way. Place the pink sheet on top of the white sheets so they stick together (you can sprinkle a bit of water in between if they're not sticking). Put the candy sheets on the prepared baking pan and allow to dry for a few hours, until the surface doesn't feel sticky. Unmold the candy, remove the parchment paper, then slice as desired and enjoy.

MAKES ABOUT 2 POUNDS

Ate de Membrillo | Quince Paste

Ates are fruit pastes made from cooked fruit and sugar, a method that was brought by the Spaniards by way of the Arabs. In the old days, the word *ate* was put at the end of the main ingredient, such as *mangate* (mango paste), *perate* (pear paste), or *membrillate* (quince paste).

Ates are cooked down in copper or heavy pots, and once cooled they are cut up into slices. The more the mixture cooks, the firmer it will be. They are sold in many markets by weight and are also cut into small cubes, tossed in sugar, and then sold in baskets of assorted flavors and colors. Known as *ates* in the majority of the country, they are also called *cajetas* (not to be confused with the caramel sauce) in some of the northern states. Quince *ate* is one of the most common flavors because of its high pectin content, and it is definitely my favorite. *Ate* can last for a long time (up to two years!). Be sure to serve it with some kind of semifirm cheese that isn't too salty (it is commonly served with Manchego).

Rinse the quinces very well, removing all the fuzz, and cover with water in a large pot. Cook over medium heat until fork-tender and the skins look like they are beginning to blister, about 30 minutes. Strain and set aside until cool enough to handle, then peel and cut into quarters, removing the seeds and any hard bits around the core.

Purée in a food processor or blender and measure the pulp. Measure the same amount of sugar and put them both in a heavy, nonreactive pot. Cook over medium heat, stirring and adjusting the heat so it's at a constant soft boil. Add the lemon juice and continue cooking, stirring once in awhile, until it is thick, you can see the pan when you scrape the spoon across the bottom, and the mixture "grabs" the spoon, up to 1½ hours. The longer it cooks, the harder it will be; if you want it a little more spreadable, cook a bit less. It will thicken more once it has cooled.

Line an 8 by 8-inch baking pan or any other mold you have with parchment paper (you can pour it directly into a decorated ceramic dish to make a really nice gift).

Pour the mixture into the pan. Let cool completely and serve sliced with cheese or use it to fill flaky turnovers (page 133).

MAKES ABOUT 2½ POUNDS

5 medium quinces
(about 2 pounds)

2 to 3 cups sugar (amount
depends on fruit pulp)

1 tablespoon freshly squeezed
lemon juice

Skull-shaped *ates*

1½ cups sugar

½ cup water

½ cup apricot preserves

3 cups whole milk

1 vanilla bean, split lengthwise

2 eggs

5 egg yolks

1 cup chestnut purée

Although the original recipe calls for making your own chestnut purée, I like to use the chestnut purée from Spain or France to make this custard because it has a wonderful nutty flavor and silkiness. I met a nun in Puebla who told me they coated the mold with a bit of butter and sugar and topped the flan with apricot jam. I took this idea and made an apricot caramel to cover the bottom of the pan, and it turned out to be an unexpectedly pleasant combination that showcased flan in a whole new way.

Combine 1 cup of the sugar and the water in a small, heavy saucepan and cook over medium heat until the sugar dissolves and turns a dark golden color (once it starts changing color, you can swirl it around so it caramelizes evenly). Remove from the heat and whisk in the apricot preserves (be careful because it may splash and steam a little). Return to the heat and continue to stir until the jam is dissolved. Divide among 8 ramekins, swirling around to coat the bottoms and sides.

Preheat the oven to 350°F.

Place the milk in a saucepan. Scrape the vanilla bean with the tip of a knife over the pan, then add the pod to the pan as well. Cook over medium heat to scald the milk. Meanwhile, combine the eggs, egg yolks, and the remaining ½ cup sugar in a large mixing bowl, and place the mixing bowl on top of a towel to keep it from wobbling while you whisk in the hot liquid. Slowly strain about ½ cup of the hot milk mixture into the egg mixture while whisking. Strain the rest of the milk and whisk gently (try to prevent excess bubbles from forming) and add the chestnut purée, whisking until it's smooth.

Place the coated ramekins, evenly spaced, in a towel-lined baking dish to prevent them from sliding. Divide the mixture among the ramekins. If there are any excess bubbles, remove them with a spoon before baking. Carefully pour hot water three-quarters of the way up the dish and cover loosely with aluminum foil. Bake until the flans are set along the edges but slightly jiggly in the center, 30 to 40 minutes. Remove from the oven and remove the ramekins with a towel or tongs. Let cool for 10 minutes, and then chill in the refrigerator for at least 6 hours (or overnight).

To unmold, warm a small, sharp knife under hot water, dry it quickly, and run it around the edges of the ramekins. Dip the bottoms of the ramekins into very hot water for about 15 seconds and unmold onto a plate. The flan can be served chilled or at room temperature.

SERVES 8

2 (14-ounce) cans condensed milk

1 (12-ounce) can evaporated goat's or cow's milk

6 tablespoons unsalted butter

2 teaspoons pure vanilla extract

Pinch of salt

Double the Flavor

You can mix and match flavors as you like, and you can do it quite simply. Pour half of the mixture into the prepared pan, stir another flavor—such as coffee extract or any kind of flavored oil with a few drops of food coloring—into the other half, then pour that on top. Alternatively, you can make two separate flavors and make half a batch of each.

Jamoncillos come in different shapes and sizes, but they are always deliciously sweet (very sweet), fudgelike candies. Some of the best I've had are prepared by the Hernandez family in Toluca. This three-generation family-run business is set up in their home. The copper pots are filled with raw cow's or goat's milk, and while some stir as it cooks down with sugar for many hours, other members of the family are busy pouring or cutting different candies out on the sunny patio. The flavors they have never cease to surprise me, including lime, pine nut, coffee, papaya, guava, and coconut, to name a few.

I wanted to include at least one candy recipe in the book that wasn't as time-consuming as the others, so this is a modern adaptation of a classic. It will definitely not be as good as the ones the Hernandez family makes, but they did inspire me to play around with a few variations that will surely please anyone with a sweet tooth.

Lightly grease a 9 by 9-inch square pan. Line the pan with a piece of parchment paper or aluminum foil, leaving about a 1-inch overhang on all sides.

Combine the condensed milk, evaporated milk, butter, vanilla, and salt in a saucepan and cook over medium heat, stirring continuously with a wooden spoon or heatproof spatula, until the mixture has thickened and starts pulling away from the sides of the pan, 20 to 30 minutes. When ready, it will slide easily out of the pan when tilted.

Pour into the prepared pan and allow to set, about 2 hours. Cut into rectangles or desired shapes.

MAKES ABOUT 2 DOZEN

VARIATION: CHOCOLATE

Add 6 tablespoons unsweetened natural cocoa powder (preferably Dutch processed) along with the other ingredients.

VARIATION: LIME

Replace the vanilla with 1 teaspoon grated lime zest and add 1 tablespoon freshly squeezed lime juice and a few drops of green food coloring (if desired) once the mixture has been removed from the heat, making sure you add them slowly and stir well so it doesn't separate.

CONTINUED

Jamoncillo de Leche (continued)

VARIATION: COFFEE

Add 2 teaspoons coffee extract along with the other ingredients.

VARIATION: COCONUT

Replace the evaporated milk with the same size can of coconut milk.

VARIATION: TEQUILA

Add 1 tablespoon white or *reposado* tequila once the mixture has been removed from the heat, making sure you add it slowly and stir well so it doesn't separate.

Mamón (Cake Layer)

8 eggs, at room temperature

1¼ cups sugar

1 teaspoon grated orange
or lime zest

1¾ cups all-purpose or pastry
flour, sifted twice

2 tablespoons unsalted
butter, melted

Mango-Almond Filling

1½ cups sugar

½ cup water

2 cups fresh mango purée
(from 3 or 4 Manila mangoes)

1½ cups almond flour

1 cup sweet sherry

2 or 3 fresh mangoes,
preferably Manila

This cake is often sliced and
dried, then dipped into hot
chocolate. It is often eaten in
a dish topped with ice cream,
or soaked in liqueur for a
simple dessert.

Antes are very old desserts that were prepared in many convents. They are similar to a layer cake and are made with *marquesote* or *mamón* (similar to a pound or génoise cake) that is soaked in syrup or liqueur, then filled with a fruit jam and colorfully adorned with fresh, dried, or crystalized fruit and often meringue and nuts. During the sixteenth and seventeenth centuries, certain sweets were eaten before a meal, which is where the name of this dessert comes from: *antes de* means "prior to."

This particular *ante* was inspired by a recipe found in a manuscript from Sor Juana Inés de la Cruz. She used mamey, which I've replaced with mango because it is much more readily available and is a wonderful combination with the ground almonds and because it still represents the cultural blend apparent in the original recipe.

Preheat the oven to 350°F. Grease and flour a 9-inch cake pan.

TO MAKE THE CAKE, beat the eggs with the sugar and zest on high speed until tripled in volume. Sprinkle ½ cup of the flour on top of the eggs and fold gently. Add the flour in two more ½-cup portions as you fold gently, then add the remaining ¼ cup flour. Add the melted butter and pour into the pan. Bake for 20 to 25 minutes, or until a toothpick inserted into the center comes out clean and the cake springs back when touched lightly. Let cool for about 5 minutes and then unmold onto a wire rack to cool completely.

TO MAKE THE FILLING, combine the sugar and water in a heavy pot and bring to a boil over medium heat. Cook, stirring, until the sugar has dissolved. Cook for about 5 minutes longer, then add the mango purée and almond flour. Adjust the heat so the mixture is at a constant soft boil and cook until it is thick like jam and grabs onto a spoon. Allow to cool completely (this can be made several days in advance and stored at room temperature).

To assemble the ante, slice the cake horizontally into 3 even layers and brush each layer with the sherry. Spread one-third of the mango filling on the bottom cake layer, spreading evenly to the edges. Place another cake layer on top, spread with the mango filling, and repeat with the last layer. Refrigerate while you prepare the fresh mangoes for decorating.

To prepare the mangoes, either peel them or cut in half with a knife as close to the pit as possible, and then scoop out the flesh. Slice as desired and arrange them on top to decorate the cake. Serve cold or at room temperature.

SERVES 10 TO 12

1 large white or
orange sweet potato

4½ cups water

Juice of 1 lime

1⅓ cups sugar

½ cup puréed fresh pineapple

Glaze

1½ cups sugar

¼ cup water

These candies were supposedly created in the Santa Clara convent in the state of Puebla and are sold everywhere in that state. They are long, cigar-shaped pieces of sugary sweet potato flavored with different fruits (mostly using flavorings and added colorings), but this is the basic recipe without any distractions. They are usually made with white sweet potato, but I prefer the flavor of the yellow or orange kind. Although it takes a couple of days to dry out, you can also serve it on a platter once it has cooled (and then you won't even have to wait to eat it) the way many desserts were served in convents, and decorate it with some fresh pineapple on top.

Put the sweet potato, whole and unpeeled, in a pot and cover it with water. Bring to a boil, then decrease the heat so it's at a constant simmer, and cook until it is fork-tender (you can steam it if you prefer). Drain the water and set aside until cool enough to handle. Peel the skin and put the flesh in a container with 4 cups of the water and the lime juice. Let stand for 1 hour (you can skip this if you are serving it on a platter). Drain and purée until smooth, using a masher or food processor.

Put the sugar and the remaining ½ cup water in a heavy-bottomed pot and cook until the sugar melts and is very bubbly. Carefully add the sweet potato and the pineapple, stirring constantly, and cook until the mixture thickens and "grabs" the spoon, 30 to 45 minutes. You want to adjust the heat so it is always bubbling a little but not too much, because you don't want to burn yourself.

Remove from the heat and beat lightly with a spoon, then let cool completely (you can transfer it to a serving platter if you aren't making the candies). Place about 2 tablespoons of the mixture on a thin, damp cloth and roll up, forming a little log about 6 inches long. Repeat with the remaining mixture, rinsing the cloth often to prevent sticking but avoiding excess moisture. Place the logs on a parchment-lined baking sheet and let dry overnight. Once the tops are completely dry, turn the candies over and let dry overnight again.

TO MAKE THE GLAZE, combine the sugar and water in a small pot and bring to a boil. Cook, stirring, until the sugar has dissolved. Remove from the heat and let cool, then brush both sides of the candies (you can also dip the candies using two forks). Return to the parchment paper and allow to set overnight once again, turning as necessary. Once they are completely dry wrap them individually in wax paper—if you're not going to eat them right away.

MAKES 10 TO 15

Buñuelos de Manzana | Apple Fritters

The apples in these treats are slightly roasted, which gives them a wonderful flavor that contrasts nicely with the crispy texture of the batter. Any kind of apple can be used, but a tart one such as Granny Smith or Crispin works great.

The sparkling apple cider enhances the apple flavor, but it can be substituted with a light beer if you prefer. Serve the fritters on their own or dip them in some warm *cajeta* (add about 2 tablespoons of rum or brandy per cup of warm *cajeta* to add a nice kick and thin it out a bit) or Natilla (page 163).

TO MAKE THE APPLES, preheat the oven to 350°F. Lightly butter a baking sheet.

Peel and core the apples. Cut into slices about ¼ inch thick and place on the baking sheet. Dollop a little butter on top of the apples. Mix the sugar with the *canela* and sprinkle on top of the apples. Drizzle the brandy all around and bake until the apples are tender but not mushy, about 25 minutes. You should be able to poke a knife through easily. Place on a wire rack and let cool completely, 30 to 40 minutes. Meanwhile, prepare the batter.

TO MAKE THE BATTER, separate the eggs, making sure you don't get any of the yolks in the whites. Mix the yolks with the cider, salt, and vegetable oil. Gradually whisk in the flour by hand. In a separate bowl, whip the egg whites, and once they start to froth and thicken, add the sugar. Continue beating until glossy, stiff peaks are formed, 5 to 10 minutes total. Carefully fold into the egg-yolk mixture. Set aside until the apples are cool. This mixture shouldn't be prepared more than an hour before using.

Pour the oil into a deep-sided pan to a depth of about 2 inches and heat to 375°F. If you don't have a thermometer, you can test the temperature by pouring a little batter into the oil; it should immediately bubble and puff. Dip the apples into the batter and lift to remove the excess. Slide into the hot oil and fry in batches until golden brown on both sides, about 2 minutes, then drain on paper bags or paper towels. Test the oil between batches, because the temperature may drop. Let cool for 5 minutes, sift confectioner's sugar on top, and enjoy.

SERVES 8

Apples

2 pounds tart apples, such as Granny Smith or Crispin (about 4 large)

¼ cup unsalted butter

2 tablespoons sugar

1 teaspoon freshly ground *canela*

3 tablespoons brandy (optional)

Batter

3 eggs, at room temperature

¾ cup sparkling apple cider or light beer

½ teaspoon salt

3 tablespoons vegetable oil

1½ cups all-purpose flour

1½ tablespoons sugar

Vegetable oil, for frying

Confectioner's sugar, for dusting

1½ cups sugar

¼ cup plus 3 tablespoons water

2 teaspoons unflavored gelatin

2 cups half-and-half

Pinch of salt

2 teaspoons orange blossom water

1 cup *crema*, chilled

Fresh orange blossoms, kumquats, or orange segments, for garnish

Although the name of this dessert says it's a cream, it's really more of a creamy gelatin with a caramel sauce like that made for flan. The orange blossom makes this simple dessert quite sophisticated. It is best made a day in advance so the flavor really comes through and it is easier to unmold.

Mix ¾ cup of the sugar and the ¼ cup of water in a small, heavy saucepan and cook over medium heat until the sugar dissolves and turns a dark golden color (once it starts changing color, you can swirl it around so it caramelizes evenly). Divide among 6 ramekins and swirl around to coat the bottoms and sides.

Add the remaining 3 tablespoons water to a small bowl and sprinkle the gelatin over. Allow to bloom or set.

Heat the half-and-half, salt, and the remaining ¾ cup sugar in a saucepan over medium heat, stirring, until the sugar dissolves. Turn off the heat and add the gelatin, stirring until dissolved. Add the orange blossom water and pour into a large bowl.

Whip the *crema* until thick and soft peaks form. Fold into the gelatin mixture, and then pour into the ramekins. Tap them very lightly so there are no air bubbles and refrigerate overnight.

When ready to serve, remove the ramekins from the refrigerator and let sit for about 10 minutes. Heat a shallow pan with water until nearly boiling, and then turn off the heat. Dip a small, sharp knife into the water and run around the sides to loosen. Dip the ramekins one at a time into the water so the caramel melts a bit, and then flip over onto a plate. Garnish with the fresh orange blossoms and serve.

SERVES 6

Gelatin the Old-Fashioned Way

In the old days, commercial gelatin wasn't available, so cooks simmered veal or pork bones in water to make it.

Mazapanes de Cacahuate | Peanut Marzipans

This recipe takes very little time to make but amazes everyone. The natural oil from the peanuts, or any other nut you are using, comes out when you grind it, and the sugar barely holds this crumbly, nutty sweetness together.

2 cups toasted unsalted peanuts, skins removed (pistachios, pecans, or almonds may be substituted)

1½ cups confectioner's sugar

Grind the peanuts in a food processor. Add the sugar and continue mixing, scraping the sides from time to time, until the peanuts release their oil and a compact paste is formed when pressed between your fingers. Be patient as this may take a bit of time depending on your food processor.

Put some of the paste into a 2-inch-diameter cookie cutter, filling it up about ¾ inch high. Press down with your hands until compacted. Remove the cutter carefully and repeat until all the paste is used. Wrap in cellophane or tissue paper like a sugar candy.

MAKES 10

Wrapping Mazapanes

To prepare the wrapper using cellophane or tissue paper, cut 10 pieces into 4 by 3-inch rectangles. Then cut thin strips of a little less than 1 inch from the short sides toward the center all the way down. Put the marzipans in the center and roll over so the candy is fully covered, then twist the ends.

MAIZ

—

CORN

THE ANCIENT PEOPLE OF MEXICO referred to corn as the "herb of the gods." This plant was the heart of the land and still is in many ways. Corn, pumpkin, beans, and chiles were cultivated in Mesoamerica starting in 7000 B.C.E., and it is incredible to realize that they are the soul of the Mexican diet to this day. When the Europeans arrived in the Americas, corn could be found everywhere, and they referred to the new lands as "corn towns" or "corn cultures," describing the distinct link between plant and man.

Fray Bernandino Sahagún wrote that the Aztecs' main sustenance was maize and that they grew the white and different-colored varieties to use as monetary units. Today, more than twenty-five types of corn are harvested in Mexico.

As written in the Popol Vuh, the sacred book of the Mayans, it was believed that man was created by Yuum Kaax, the god of corn. The Nahuas said that Quetzalcoatl, the feathered serpent deity, transformed into an ant to steal the sacred corn and give it to the humans for food.

This is why the first *mazorcas* (corn cobs) were given as an offering to Cinteotl, the young god of maize.

Many ceremonial rites were created to bless the harvest of corn and its various deities. The Aztecs made idols of different gods using corn and other grains, at times binding them with some of the blood from the sacrificed men, who were eaten during certain rituals. The Tzotziles, an indigenous group from the Chiapas region, have a tradition where they cut the umbilical cord of a newborn over a *mazorca*. The blood-covered corn is then planted during the next harvest season so that there is continuity in the community.

Today, there are offerings of *aguardiente* (a distilled beverage), coffee, and flowers all around Mexico before the corn is harvested. One of the biggest offerings takes place in Metepec during the feast of San Isidro Labrador, the patron of the harvest.

Mexicans utilize every part of the corn in one way or another. The *xiotes* (tender young corn) are eaten whole and mainly consumed by farmworkers. Corn kernels are eaten as a vegetable in soups and stews and ground to make tortillas and masa for an incredible variety of *antojitos*, tamales, sauces, and beverages such as *tesgüiño* (a fermented corn beverage), which is used in many wedding celebrations. *Tomochtly* (the green leaves) are used to feed different animals and as part of compost. Corn silks are dried, then steeped and used as a home remedy for stomachaches and as a natural diuretic. The *totomoxtle* (dried leaves) are used as fuel, to wrap foods such as cheese and tamales, to roll up tobacco, and to make figurines that are part of the *arte popular*. Even the worms from the butterflies that lay their eggs on the *mazorcas* are eaten.

A Mayan saying claims that "corn is the grace of God," and in a way, eating corn has been a way of preserving Mexican culture. It is inconceivable to think of Mexico without corn, and the sweet preparations we make from it are only a small fraction of its indelible richness.

Palomitas Acarameladas | Caramel Popcorn Balls

Popcorn has been eaten in Mexico since pre-Hispanic times and has remained a favorite snack when combined with the sweet molassy flavor of *piloncillo*. The butter in the caramel makes the sweetness of the honey and *piloncillo* come together. This recipe isn't time consuming but requires close attention because the caramel can burn in seconds if you're not careful.

Grease a baking sheet or line it with a nonstick mat.

Heat the oil in a pot over medium heat and add the kernels. Cover the pot and cook, shaking the pot lightly, until all the corn is popped, about 5 minutes. Pour into a stainless steel bowl.

Combine the butter, *piloncillo*, and honey in a medium-large pot with a candy thermometer clipped onto the side and cook over medium heat, stirring constantly until it boils, then continue to cook, stirring only occasionally and making sure it doesn't stick, until it reaches the hard-crack stage (300°F, see page 13). Add the salt and baking soda, stirring rapidly and carefully. Immediately pour the caramel onto the popcorn. Toss quickly to coat and pour onto the prepared baking sheet. Use lightly oiled spoons or gloves to form the balls while the caramel is still warm. Allow to cool, then enjoy. These are best eaten the day they are made.

MAKES 10 TO 15

2 tablespoons vegetable oil

⅓ cup popcorn kernels

½ cup unsalted butter

1 cup chopped *piloncillo* or firmly packed dark brown sugar

½ cup honey

½ teaspoon salt

½ teaspoon baking soda

Tamales de Pasitas con Nuez | Sweet Tamales with Raisins and Pecans

25 dried cornhusks

1 cup water

1½ cups masa harina

½ cup lard, vegetable shortening, or butter, softened

1 cup firmly packed light brown sugar

¼ to ½ cup whole milk

Pinch of salt

1½ teaspoons baking powder

1 teaspoon freshly ground *canela*

½ cup toasted coarsely chopped pecans

¾ cup dark raisins

1 ounce *acitrón* or candied pineapple, finely diced

Red food coloring (optional)

Corn tamales have prevailed for at least five centuries as ubiquitous protagonists in ceremonies and rituals such as Día de los Muertos. This preparation is from Durango, and I want to thank Ricardo Gurrola for providing me with the recipe. They go deliciously well with Strawberry Atole (page 29).

Rinse the cornhusks, place them in a bowl, and cover with boiling water for at least half an hour, or until they are soft (put a plate on top and weight it with a large can to keep them submerged).

Bring the water to a boil and combine with the masa harina, stirring until smooth. Reserve.

Beat the lard with a wooden spoon or in a mixer with the paddle attachment until smooth. Add the brown sugar and half of the masa. Beat for about 30 seconds, add a little bit of the milk, then alternate adding milk and the rest of the masa, beating after each addition and adding enough milk so the mixture is thick but still pourable. Add the salt and baking powder, beat for a couple of minutes, and then test the dough by putting a bit of the batter in a glass filled with cold water. The batter should float. If it doesn't, continue beating until it does. Beat in the *canela*, pecans, raisins, *acitrón*, and a few drops of red food coloring until just combined.

Drain the cornhusks and scoop about ¼ cup of the batter into a husk, spreading it with the back of a spoon into a rectangle and leaving at least 1 inch all around (a little more on the long sides). If the husks are too small or broken, put two together and overlap them. Fold one of the long sides toward the center, and then fold the other long side on top. Tuck the exposed sides underneath; if they are still too small, wrap the tamale in another husk and tie it with a thin strip of husk (this isn't necessary but is just an extra precaution). Repeat to use up all the batter.

Fill a pot with enough hot water to reach just underneath, but not touching, a steamer (you can use the collapsible kind if you don't have a special pot). Cover the bottom of the steamer with leftover cornhusks and arrange the tamales vertically, standing them up so they rest against one another. Cover with any remaining leaves or scraps, cover with a lid, and cook over medium heat until the tamales slide out of the wrappers, 1 to 1½ hours. Add more boiling water to the bottom pot to make sure water reaches the bottom of the steamer. Serve warm. The tamales can be cooled and stored in the freezer, wrapped tightly, for up to 3 months.

MAKES ABOUT 1 DOZEN

30 dried cornhusks

1 cup unsalted butter, at room temperature

½ cup vegetable shortening

1½ cups sugar

2 cups masa harina

Green food coloring (optional)

2 cups whole milk

2 tablespoons grated lime zest

Pinch of salt

Testing Tamales

There is a theory that many home cooks firmly believe in. To test whether the dough has been beaten enough and is ready to be put in the husks, put a bit of dough in a glass filled with cold water. If it begins to float, it's ready and you can be sure that your tamales will be light and fluffy. If it doesn't, just beat a bit longer.

For a few years now, my dad and his partner Manuel have made an incredible Día de los Muertos celebration in a country house located near Cuernavaca. They invite friends and neighbors, attempting to preserve the culture that many children in big cities confuse or associate nowadays with Halloween. Hundreds of assorted tamales and hot chocolate are always made to welcome the guests as they come to visit the awesome *ofrenda*. One year, Mrs. Catalina, the charming woman responsible for the tamale feast, kindly showed me how to make them (although she didn't let me touch the batter because she said it would separate). The lime zest ones were my absolute favorite and remind me of a very light and airy sponge cake. The bit of shortening helps give it a wonderful texture, but you may substitute more butter if you prefer.

Rinse the cornhusks under cold water, place them in a bowl, and cover with boiling water (put a plate on top and weight it with a large can to keep them submerged). Let sit for at least 30 minutes, or until soft.

In a bowl, combine the butter, shortening, and sugar with your hands or in a mixer with the paddle attachment until very creamy. Add the masa and mix well (it'll look a bit like coarse meal). Combine a few drops of the food coloring with 3 tablespoons of the milk, then add that and the rest of the milk gradually while mixing until incorporated. Stir in the lime zest and salt.

Drain the cornhusks and scoop about ¼ cup of the batter into a husk, spreading it with the back of a spoon and leaving at least 1 inch all around (a little more on the long sides). If the husks are too small or broken, put two together and overlap them. Fold one of the long sides toward the center, and then fold the other long side on top. Tuck the exposed sides underneath; if they are still too small, wrap the tamale in another husk and tie it with a thin strip of husk (this isn't necessary but is just an extra precaution). Repeat to use up all the batter.

Fill a pot with enough hot water to reach just underneath, but not touching, a steamer (you can use the collapsible kind if you don't have a special pot). Cover the bottom of the steamer with leftover cornhusks and arrange the tamales vertically, standing them up so they rest against one another. Cover with any remaining leaves or scraps, cover with a lid, and cook over medium heat until the tamales slide out of the wrappers, 1 to 1½ hours. Add more boiling water to the bottom pot as needed to make sure water reaches the bottom of the steamer. Serve warm. The tamales can be stored in the freezer, wrapped tightly, for up to 3 months.

MAKES ABOUT 2 DOZEN

Tamal de Fresa | Strawberry Tamales

You can find all sorts of corn flour (masa harina) in Mexico, and their colors can seem almost fake. The best place to find them is the food mills, and they are commonly found near markets. Whenever I can, I like to make this dish with pink or blue corn because it enhances the color in a natural way and it somehow seems more fun.

Rinse the cornhusks under cold water, place them in a bowl, and cover with boiling water (put a plate on top and weight it with a large can to keep them submerged). Let sit for at least 30 minutes, or until soft.

Wash the strawberries, dry them, and remove any green parts with the tip of a knife. Put them in a bowl and mash with your hands or a potato masher, then add the vanilla and salt. You want them to still be a bit chunky. Set aside.

In a bowl, combine the butter, shortening, sugar, and baking powder with a handheld mixer or in a mixer with the paddle attachment and blend until very creamy. Add the masa harina and mix well (it'll look a bit like coarse meal). Continue to mix, adding a bit of the milk and alternating with the mashed strawberries until fully combined.

Drain the cornhusks and scoop about ¼ cup of the batter into a husk, spreading it with the back of a spoon and leaving at least 1 inch all around (a little more on the long sides). If the husks are too small or broken, put two together and overlap them. Fold one of the long sides toward the center, and then fold the other long side on top. Tuck the exposed sides underneath; if they are still too small, wrap the tamale in another husk and tie it with a thin strip of husk (this isn't necessary but is just an extra precaution). Repeat to use up all the batter.

Fill a pot with enough hot water to reach just underneath, but not touching, a steamer (you can use the collapsible kind if you don't have a special pot). Cover the bottom of the steamer with leftover cornhusks and arrange the tamales vertically, standing them up so they rest against one another. Cover with any remaining leaves or scraps, cover with a lid, and cook over medium heat until the tamales slide out of the wrappers, 1 to 1½ hours. Add more boiling water to the bottom pot as needed to make sure water reaches the bottom of the steamer. Serve warm. The tamales can be cooled and stored in the freezer, wrapped tightly, for up to 3 months.

MAKES ABOUT 2 DOZEN

30 dried cornhusks

1 pint fresh strawberries

½ teaspoon pure vanilla extract

Pinch of salt

1 cup unsalted butter, at room temperature

½ cup vegetable shortening

1 cup sugar

½ teaspoon baking powder

2 cups blue or white masa harina

1¼ cups whole milk

1 pound leaf lard (see page 11)
or vegetable shortening

1½ cups sugar

2 eggs

2 cups masa harina

1 cup all-purpose flour

¾ cups freshly brewed coffee

These cookies from Tamaulipas get their crunchy texture from the lard and the corn flour. They are rarely glazed, but you may choose to brush a beaten egg white and dust with sugar before baking them as I like to do.

Beat the lard with a wooden spoon or in a mixer using the paddle attachment until smooth. Add the sugar and mix until light and fluffy. Add the eggs, one at a time, then add one-third of the flour. Add about one-third of the coffee and continue alternating the flour and coffee in two more batches until incorporated. Scrape down the sides as necessary and beat until thoroughly combined. Turn out onto a lightly floured surface and knead until a smooth and uniform dough is formed.

With your hands, roll out pieces about 5 inches wide and ½ inch thick, starting in the center and rolling outward so that they are evenly thick. Connect one end of each piece to the other, making a ring, and place on a parchment-lined baking sheet, about 1 inch apart. Refrigerate until firm, about 10 minutes.

Preheat the oven to 350°F. Bake the cookies for 14 to 16 minutes, or until golden, and allow to cool on the baking sheet.

MAKES ABOUT 3 DOZEN

NOTE: You can substitute milk for the coffee and 2 teaspoons aniseed in the mixture to prepare the *pemoles* the way they do in many parts of Veracruz.

Gorditas de Piloncillo | Sweet Fried Masa Cakes

2 ounces finely chopped *piloncillo*

3 ounces queso añejo
or ricotta salata

1 teaspoon freshly ground *canela*

1 pound fresh masa, or
1⅔ cups masa harina mixed
with 1 cup hot water

Lard or vegetable oil, for frying
(about 2 cups)

The name *gorditas* is used in an endearing manner to describe many small but "fatty" (referring to the thickness) foods. Everyone loves *gorditas*, and there are many different kinds. I tried these in Nuevo Leon and love them because they are fried, which makes them (or me) double *gordita*. I also like them because of the salty cheese and *piloncillo* that make them go wonderfully with a hot chocolate (page 25) or *champurrado* (page 22).

Combine the *piloncillo*, cheese, and *canela* in a bowl and knead in the masa until uniformly distributed. Add a bit of water if it feels too dry or a little masa harina if it's too sticky. Shape the dough into 12 even balls.

Place enough lard in a heavy pot to reach a depth of least 3 inches and heat to about 365°F. (You can check the temperature by dipping a wooden spoon in the fat; once it steadily bubbles, it's ready.) While this heats, flatten the masa rounds between your hands (you can dampen your hands very lightly so they don't stick or press down on top with a piece of plastic wrap) to about ⅛ inch thick. Slide them into the hot fat and bathe them with a spoon so they are covered with fat at all times, and turn often, frying until they are golden on all sides and make sure not to overcrowd the pan. Drain on paper bags or towels and enjoy warm. (You can keep them in a warming oven for 15 minutes.)

MAKES 1 DOZEN

Dulce de Maiz Azul | Blue Corn Dessert

8 ounces ground blue corn

4 cups boiling water

1¼ cups granulated sugar

4 cups whole milk

1 vanilla bean, split lengthwise

Pinch of salt

⅓ cup raw sugar

Many desserts in Mexico are cooked on the stove and served on a platter at room temperature. This particular one is from the State of Mexico and is prepared for Día de los Muertos celebrations. You can find ground blue corn at many specialty markets or online (see Sources), or you can substitute it for the white variety.

Put the ground corn in a bowl. Pour the boiling water over the corn, whisking until dissolved; strain. Place the corn mixture in a large pot with the granulated sugar, milk, vanilla bean (scrape it with the tip of a knife and add it with the pod), and salt. Cook it at a soft simmer,

CONTINUED

stirring occasionally, until the mixture has thickened and you can see the bottom of the pot when scraped with a spoon, about 1 hour. It will have a porridge-like consistency. Discard the vanilla bean, pour onto a serving platter or individual bowls, and sprinkle the raw sugar all over. Serve warm or at room temperature (place a thin piece of plastic directly on top to prevent a crust from forming if you'll be eating it later).

SERVES 8 TO 10

Pan de Elote | Corn Bread

As weird as it may sound, whenever I think of these, I think of the trunk of a car. You see, parked around the streets of Mexico City are numerous cars filled with towers of corn breads. Their trunks are open and there is a cardboard sign announcing the delicacies for sale. This particular recipe takes only a few minutes to prepare (plus baking time, of course) and the result is very tasty and moist. Enjoy a slice with a cup of cold milk or coffee.

Preheat the oven to 325°F. Grease and flour a 9-inch cake pan.

Slice the kernels from the corn over a kitchen towel so they don't fly all over the place.

Sift together the flour and the baking soda. Put the eggs, condensed milk, *crema*, and vanilla in an electric blender or food processor and mix to combine. Slice the butter into small pats, then add it to the blender. Add the flour mixture and the corn kernels, then blend until it's well incorporated (the mixture will not be completely smooth and that's okay).

Pour the batter into the prepared pan and bake until a toothpick inserted into the center comes out clean, 35 to 40 minutes. Let cool slightly, invert onto a wire rack, and allow to cool. Cut into slices and enjoy warm or at room temperature.

SERVES 8 TO 10

5 ears of corn, shucked (about 2 cups kernels)

3 tablespoons rice flour or all-purpose flour, plus extra for the pan

1½ teaspoons baking powder

5 eggs, at room temperature

1 (14-ounce) can condensed milk

⅓ cup *crema* or sour cream

½ teaspoon pure vanilla extract

½ cup (4 ounces) unsalted butter at room temperature, plus a little extra for the pan

1 cup sugar

¼ cup water

2 large ears white corn, shucked

1 (14-ounce) can condensed milk

1 tablespoon cornstarch

5 eggs

2 cups whole milk

1 teaspoon pure vanilla extract

¼ teaspoon salt

Although this is not one of the most traditional recipes, I have seen it in different areas of the country, probably because it combines two of our favorite things: corn and flan.

Most of the corn flans I have tasted are made with condensed milk, so I've tried to recreate that flavor and texture. Make this with white corn at the peak of the season to ensure that the flavor really comes through.

Preheat the oven to 350°F. Combine the sugar and water in a small, heavy saucepan. Cover and bring to a boil over medium-low heat, then remove the lid to release the steam, which will help avoid crystallization. Continue cooking until the sugar dissolves and turns a dark golden color, then swirl the mixture around so it caramelizes evenly. Divide among 6 ramekins and swirl around to coat the bottoms.

Slice the kernels from the corn and set aside. Place the condensed milk, cornstarch, eggs, whole milk, vanilla, and salt in a blender and blend until smooth. Add the corn kernels and blend until combined (it will be a little grainy).

Place the prepared ramekins, evenly spaced, on a towel-lined baking dish to keep them from sliding. Divide the flan mixture among the ramekins and pop any bubbles with a spoon. Carefully pour hot water to fill three-fourths of the way up the baking dish and cover loosely with aluminum foil (you can also make a few holes in the foil to prevent steaming). Bake until the flans are set around the edges but slightly jiggly in the center, about 30 minutes. Remove the baking dish from the oven and remove the ramekins with a towel or tongs. Let cool, uncovered, until cool to the touch, then chill in the refrigerator for at least 6 hours (this can be done a day in advance).

To unmold, fill a bowl or small pot with 2 to 3 inches of very hot water. Dip a small, sharp knife into the hot water, dry it quickly, and run it around the edges of the ramekins. Dip the bottoms of the ramekins into the hot water for about 20 seconds and unmold onto a plate. It should slowly unmold, but if it feels a bit stuck, run a knife around the edges once again. Serve chilled or at room temperature.

SERVES 6

DULCES DE ANTAÑO

—

HEIRLOOM SWEETS

MANY COOKBOOKS THAT I HAVE FOUND in Mexico, some dating back to the eighteenth century, are handwritten manuscripts. They are a collection of recipes but also a guide for traditional life. Candy making in Mexico is also part of a strong cultural and oral tradition that has transmitted customs and recipes from generation to generation, like family jewels.

Most of the art of candy making was taught in small schools for indigenous and mestizo girls and teens, and later on, in convents. In time, the teachings left the cloisters and found their way onto the streets, traveling to villages and towns and finding a home in many backyards and kitchens.

Patiently and with devotion, many a cook stirred these sweet concoctions in copper and clay pots, strained them through fine-mesh sieves, poured them into handmade molds, and shaped them into wonderful, delicate deliciousness. They were often served on handcrafted platters made from *talavera*, ceramic, or silver. Eventually, some of these candy artisans went out onto the streets to sell their handiwork, singing creative poems and rhymes to lure customers: *Si no me compras el dulce mi amor, te come el tlacuache* ("If you don't buy my sweets, my love, the opossum will eat you").

This widespread distribution allowed for much creativity and sentimental pride; candy making became a source of personal expression through taste and sensibility. The natural surroundings gave birth to many confections, and these are usually referred to as *dulces regionales* or *típicos*, whereby each region is defined by certain sweets.

Puebla is perhaps the place most famous for *dulces típicos*. Along the Calle 6 Oriente—also referred to as Santa Clara (alluding to the convent by the same name on that street) or, colloquially, as *calle de los dulces* (the sweets street)—are many, many shops filled with marvelous candies stacked next to one another. The city is known for many sweets, particularly its *tortitas de Santa Clara* (round cookies with a silky pumpkin seed center; below left) and *camotes* (candied sweet potato cylinders).

There are many other wonderful places that stand out as well. In Morelia, Michoacán, there is even a small museum devoted to the candies from the region; Córdoba, Veracruz, is renowned for coconut and almond candies and various crystallized fruits; and the *alegrías* (puffed amaranth candy) made in Xochimilco are celebrated in a yearly festival.

Another incredible festival takes place in Toluca and lasts from mid-October to the beginning of November. This one features *alfeñiques*, elaborate and colorful figurines made from almond, pumpkin seed paste, and/or sugar; they are most often made in the shapes of animals and items that allude to death, such as coffins and skulls. Their preparation is delicate and time-consuming, so artisans begin months in advance; it is quite a spectacle to see.

The incredible artistry of these heirloom sweets is not just limited to the ingredients, however. It is apparent in the skillful and patiently crafted fondant decorations of *calaveritas* (sugar skulls); in the ornate candy hearts, crosses, and coffins; in the delicate paper wrappings in bright colors; and in the beautiful displays, whether it's a cart, a modest platform or stand, a hand-woven basket filled with a marvelous selection of candies, or a store's windows exhibiting exquisite towers of bright, crystallized oranges and symmetrically balanced logs of caramel.

Handmade artisan candy is not limited to shops and markets, either. Hawkers sell fluorescent pink meringues outside certain restaurants and on particular street corners. Likewise, *dulceros ambulantes* or *callejeros* sell their sweets in city parks. Many announce their arrival with a percussive triangle, a humorous saying, or a melodic whistle. Yet some of the best ones are hidden away, made in homes and sold only to a privileged few—if you know where to look. Wherever heirloom sweets are found in Mexico, they are greeted with tender emotion for the cultural richness that has come down through the ages.

1 cup dried pinto or kidney beans, picked and rinsed

2 quarts water

1 (3-inch) piece *canela*

½ teaspoon salt

2 cups sugar

2 cups freshly squeezed orange juice

1 teaspoon grated orange zest

¾ cup currants

½ cup sugar plus 1 teaspoon freshly ground *canela*

I know you're probably thinking, bean candy? That doesn't sound too good. I was doubtful, too, but I was pleasantly surprised and excited about this wonderful recipe. I am deeply grateful to our dear family friend Amado for getting this recipe that came from his friend.

The beans are cooked with cinnamon, puréed, and cooked again with orange juice and sugar. After awhile of stirring, the flavors begin to come together and a wonderful chestnutlike texture is achieved. The paste is then formed into balls and rolled in sugar. I love giving it to people to try and guess what the main ingredient is. Although only one person out of about thirty is able to guess, they all really like it. The original recipe is made with dark raisins, but I prefer to use currants.

Cover the beans with abundant cold water and soak overnight. Drain and put the beans in a medium pot with the water and *canela*. Bring to a boil and adjust the heat so it's at a constant soft simmer; cook until tender, 60 to 75 minutes, adding more water if necessary. Add the salt and remove from the heat. Let cool, then purée in a food processor together with any remaining liquid (no more than 1 cup).

Combine the sugar, orange juice, and zest in a medium pot and cook until slightly syrupy, 10 to 15 minutes. Add the puréed beans and cook, stirring continuously, over medium-low heat, until there is no more liquid and you can see the bottom of the pot when you stir, 30 to 45 minutes. The mixture will be thick and will hold onto a spoon when you lift it. Stir in the currants and let sit until cool enough to handle.

Using about 1 tablespoon of the mixture, roll into gumball-size balls, and then roll in the cinnamon-sugar mixture. Let cool completely before serving.

MAKES 4 DOZEN

Alegrías | Amaranth "Happiness" Candy

Legend has it that this "happiness" candy got its name in the middle of the sixteenth century, when Fray Martín de Valencia prepared a mixture of puffed amaranth seeds and honey; when the indigenous people tried it, they were so happy they began to sing, dance, and play music like they did in many pre-Hispanic rituals and continue to do in the yearly *alegría* festival that takes place in Tulyehualco.

Alegría remains one of the oldest candies in Mexico, but it is now made with sugar or honey and *piloncillo*. In the tropical climates of Veracruz, I tried some incredibly crispy ones, which really surprised me because of the humidity of the region; a man who has been making these treats for more than forty years told me that his trick was to add some glucose. This wonderful nutritious and historical candy is shaped into rounds or blocks and is often decorated with nuts, pumpkin seeds, and raisins, as I have done here.

Line a baking sheet with parchment paper. Combine the pecans, peanuts, raisins, and pumpkin seeds in a bowl and spread on the prepared pan.

Combine the *piloncillo*, honey, and lemon juice in a medium pot over medium heat and cook until the *piloncillo* has melted and the mixture has thickened slightly, 5 to 10 minutes. Remove from the heat and add the amaranth seeds, stirring quickly to mix everything well. Pour into the pan with the nuts and seeds, and carefully press down with slightly damp hands (so you don't burn yourself) to compact the mixture.

Allow to cool completely, 30 to 40 minutes at least, then invert onto a cutting board. Cut the mixture into the desired shapes with a sharp knife. If it seems to be sticking to the knife, simply dip the knife into hot water, dry, and continue cutting.

If you have any leftover *alegrías* (I doubt you will), wrap them in plastic wrap, place in a tightly sealed container, and store in a cool, dry area for up to 3 weeks.

MAKES ABOUT 2 DOZEN

NOTE: These are best made on days and in locations that are not too humid; if you happen to live in an area where it is always hot, add 2 tablespoons glucose to the honey mixture.

½ cup chopped toasted pecans

½ cup lightly toasted peanuts

½ cup dark raisins

½ cup lightly toasted pumpkin seeds

8 ounces chopped *piloncillo*

½ cup honey

½ teaspoon freshly squeezed lemon or lime juice

4 ounces puffed amaranth seeds

Amaranth Seeds in Pre-Hispanic Times

In pre-Hispanic times, the Aztecs used amaranth seeds to make statues of their gods for ceremonies and rituals, binding them with blood. When the conquerors arrived, they tried to eliminate their use because it conflicted with Christianity.

Melcocha de Pepitas | Pumpkin Seed Nougat

I remember the first time I tried these treats. I may not know exactly where I was or how young I was, but I do remember the sweet smile and *piloncillo*-colored eyes of the lady who sold them to me; I remember her braided hair intertwined with yellow ribbons and can almost feel the touch of her hand as she handed me the white fluffy, shiny cloud on a thin piece of banana leaf. I remember trying it and loving it.

Be sure to read the recipe all the way through before you begin. You can also choose to cut the nougat into pieces. In that case, spread the mixture with a moistened spatula over the banana leaf or a nonstick mat, allow to dry, and cut into the desired size.

Preheat the oven to 350°F. Unfold the banana leaves, lightly wipe them with a cloth, and cut into 5-inch squares or circles using scissors (not a knife). Lay at least 2 dozen on a couple of baking sheets, but have a few extra just in case.

Lay the pumpkin seeds in a single layer on a parchment paper–lined baking sheet and toast in the oven until they are only very slightly brown around the edges, 4 to 6 minutes. Turn off the oven but leave them inside.

Combine the sugar, water, corn syrup, and vanilla in a small saucepan and set aside. Pour the honey into a separate saucepan, place over medium-low heat, and attach a candy thermometer to the side of the pan (you may need to tilt it slightly to be able to read it). Place the egg whites in the bowl of a stand mixer or use a handheld mixer. Once the honey reaches 226°F, start whipping the egg whites on high speed and continue cooking the honey until it reaches 248°F, about 4 minutes.

Immediately put the pot with the sugar mixture over the heat, transferring the clean thermometer to it. Drizzle the hot honey in a stream into the egg whites, while continuing to whip on high speed. Cook the sugar mixture until it reaches 298°F, 5 to 7 minutes. Slowly pour the sugar mixture into the egg whites (if you do it too fast the whites will collapse), while you continue to whip on high speed. Once you have added all the sugar, whip for 2 to 3 minutes longer. Remove the bowl from the mixer and fold in the pumpkin seeds by hand, reserving about ½ cup to top.

Spoon 2 to 3 tablespoons of the mixture onto each banana leaf, using the back of the spoon to spread it. Dip the spoon lightly into hot water as needed to prevent sticking, but make sure the spoon is not too wet. Sprinkle the reserved pumpkin seeds over the surface. Allow to set for 2 hours. Store in an airtight container in a dry cool place for about

1 package (about 30) banana leaves

3 cups raw unsalted pumpkin seeds

¾ cup sugar

½ cup water

3 tablespoons corn syrup

¼ teaspoon pure vanilla extract

¾ cup honey

2 egg whites, at room temperature

3 weeks. If you need to stack them, make sure each nougat is sandwiched between 2 banana leaves.

NOTE: The temperature that you need to cook the sugar to in the recipe, as with most candymaking, is crucial to obtaining the desired texture—a couple of degrees difference can really change the outcome. Also, avoid making them on humid days so the nougat is able to dry out properly.

Gaznates | Fritters Filled with Mezcal-Flavored Meringue

A *gaznate* is a crunchy cylinder filled with a very sweet and airy meringue. They were carefully stacked into a tower and commonly sold outside movie theaters. The meringue is either left white or tinted a fluorescent pink and is commonly flavored with *pulque* (a fermented alcoholic beverage made from the maguey plant), which many believe is essential. *Pulque* is practically impossible to get outside Mexico, so I made my version with mezcal.

You will need noncorrosive metal tubes, which you can buy at many cooking stores or online, for wrapping the dough and frying it. Or follow the alternative method below if you can't find the tubes.

⅓ cup all-purpose flour

¼ teaspoon baking powder

4 egg yolks

1 tablespoon confectioner's sugar

¼ cup brandy or rum

Vegetable oil, for frying

1 recipe Italian Meringue (use filling variation, page 144)

Combine the flour and baking powder in a bowl. In a separate bowl, beat the egg yolks lightly, then add the flour mixture and sugar and stir to combine. Add the brandy gradually and beat until a smooth, uniform dough is achieved. Cover with plastic wrap and let sit for 10 minutes.

Turn out onto a lightly floured surface and roll out into a paper-thin rectangle, then cut into 12 rectangles. Roll onto metal tubes and dab the seams with a little water so they stick together. (If you don't have metal tubes, wrap the dough around a ball of aluminum foil, and keep them open in the fryer using a chopstick or skewer.)

Pour oil into a heavy skillet to a depth of 4 inches and heat to 350°F. Fry the *gaznates* until golden brown, 3 to 4 minutes, turning them carefully to fry evenly. Drain on paper bags or towels, allow to cool slightly, and then remove the metal tubes. (These can be made a day in advance without filling them.)

Prepare the meringue as directed. When the meringue is cool, pipe it into the fried cylinders, making sure they are filled evenly all the way through (if you don't have a piping bag, use a resealable plastic bag and cut off one corner). Serve immediately.

MAKES 1 DOZEN

How the Gaznate Got Its Name

This confection is named after the *gaznate*, or windpipe, because it is similar in shape.

Merengues Ruta Maya | Lime Meringues

Whenever I think of meringues in Mexico, I think of big crunchy pillows adorned with sliced almonds and imagine my shirt filled with crumbs as I hold it in my hand, eager to reach the center that cradles little threads of chewiness. These meringues are a direct import from the French with no real adaptations. In the Mayan region (Quintana Roo, Yucatan, and Campeche) however, the meringues are a more delicate matter. They have a slightly crunchy exterior and a very soft, cottonlike interior perfumed with lime zest and sweetened with a lot of sugar. I was very curious about how these particular meringues were made and visited the home of Geny Beatriz Camal Ruiz, a candy artisan in Bacalar, Quintana Roo. Beatriz begins preparing her candies at 3:00 or 4:00 in the morning so that she is ready by 9:00 A.M. (after she has fed her children and husband, showered, and cleaned her house) to fill her cart and go to the center of Chetumal and sell her sweet treats.

Geny, like many other candy makers of the region, uses lime zest to avoid an unpleasant eggy taste that often occurs because of the heat. Spoonfuls of batter are gently placed on top of an aluminum tub with a little water to prevent sticking. She then places a *comal* on top of the tub and hot charcoal on top of it. This way, the meringue cooks from top to bottom, leaving the center soft and seemingly uncooked. The coal provides a wonderful smoky background but does not distract from the vibrant lime zest.

I tried to do these in a home kitchen with terrible results and am very grateful that Nick Malgieri, a wonderful and sweet pastry chef, was able to help me out and achieve the texture I was looking for. You will need five baking sheets for this recipe, so borrow some if you don't have enough.

3 egg whites, at room temperature

⅔ cup sugar

¼ teaspoon cream of tartar

Pinch of salt

1 teaspoon freshly grated lime zest

Bring a pot of water to a simmer on the stove top. Line 2 baking sheets with parchment paper.

Place the egg whites, sugar, cream of tartar, and salt in a very clean, very dry bowl (if you have a stand mixer, use that bowl for this part) over the pot of simmering water (the water shouldn't touch the bowl). Whisk until the sugar has dissolved and the egg whites feel warm (not hot) to the touch.

Remove from the heat and whip at medium-high speed until starting to thicken, then add the lime zest and whip until you have glossy, high peaks.

Scoop the meringue into a pastry bag (or use a resealable plastic bag and cut off one corner) and pipe 1-inch kisses onto the 2 prepared baking sheets, leaving about ½ inch between them. Let sit at room temperature until a slight crust has formed on the outside, 1 to 1½ hours.

Preheat the oven to 300°F and position the rack in the top third of the oven.

Stack 3 baking sheets then place the baking sheet with the meringues on top of them. Bake until the meringues feel dry, 10 to 15 minutes. Remove the baking sheet with the meringues and repeat with the second batch. While these are in the oven, stick together 2 of the baked meringues by lightly pressing the flat sides against one another (the inside should be soft and pillowy, almost raw-like). Repeat with the rest of the meringues once they come out of the oven and let cool completely. These should be eaten the day they are made.

MAKES ABOUT 2 DOZEN

Palanquetas | Brittles

3 cups sugar

½ cup water

⅔ cup light corn syrup

6 tablespoons unsalted butter

2½ cups nuts or seeds (pumpkin seeds, peanuts, sesame seeds, and almonds are common choices)

1 teaspoon baking soda

1 teaspoon salt

Brittles in Mexico are made with honey, *piloncillo*, all sorts of nuts, and sesame seeds. There are different kinds depending on the area, but overall they tend to be a bit too hard so I like to add a little butter and baking soda, which gives them a wonderful crunch without breaking your jaw. The brittle can also be ground in a food processor and used to top ice cream.

Line a baking sheet with a nonstick mat or grease it, and lightly grease an offset metal spatula (so that the brittle will be easier to spread).

Combine the sugar, water, corn syrup, and butter in a heavy pot over medium heat and cook, stirring, until it starts to boil. Add the nuts (pumpkin seeds will "pop") and continue cooking until you obtain a golden caramel color. Remove from the heat and add the baking soda and salt. Stir rapidly, being careful not to burn yourself from the steam, and then pour onto the prepared pan. Spread rapidly to your desired thickness. Let cool, and then break apart with your hands if it is thin or cut with an oiled knife into desired shapes. (If you choose to cut the brittle into shapes, do so while it is cooling but still somewhat warm. Once the brittle is completely cool it will break.) These can be stored in an airtight container in a cool, dry area. Use pieces of parchment paper between them so they don't stick to eack other. They will keep for a few weeks.

MAKES 2½ POUNDS

Mueganos | Sticky-Sweet Fritter Balls

Imagine a sticky, messy, sweet, syrupy, crunchy ball. It's the kind of sweet dentists warn you about (my dad has endured many painful visits to such because he absolutely loves them). They are sold by street vendors outside bus and subway stations, churches, and movie theaters; in parks, at festivals, and occasionally in candy shops. I never met anyone who actually makes these, and I found very few recipes, because, as with many sweets in Mexico, we tend to buy from people who have made a particular candy for generations. I want to thank Jose Luis Curiel, a wonderful professor and historian, for giving me this recipe.

Combine the *piloncillo*, water, and vinegar in a saucepan and bring to a boil over high heat. Lower the heat and continue cooking until the *piloncillo* has dissolved and the mixture reaches a honey-like consistency. Set aside.

Cream together the butter and sugar with an electric mixer or in a bowl with a wooden spoon. In a separate bowl, combine the flour and salt, then add to the butter mixture gradually and beat until a uniform dough is formed. Cover with plastic wrap and let rest for 10 minutes at room temperature.

Meanwhile, heat the oil in a heavy, deep pan over medium heat to 375°F. Turn the dough out onto a lightly floured surface and roll out into a square or rectangle about ⅛ inch thick. Cut into 1-inch squares.

Fry the dough in batches until lightly golden, 3 to 5 minutes. Transfer with a slotted spoon to a paper bag or paper towel to drain. Repeat until all the dough is fried.

Put the drained fried dough in the syrup and stir well to coat all the squares. Once coated, take them out with a slotted spoon or spider and place 6 to 8 mounds on a wire rack. Carefully press together with your hands to form balls (this can be a sticky situation, so you may want to wear gloves). Allow the *mueganos* to set for 5 minutes before serving.

SERVES 6

1 pound *piloncillo*, finely chopped, or 2 cups firmly packed dark brown sugar

2 cups water

2 tablespoons white vinegar

3½ tablespoons unsalted butter, at room temperature

1 tablespoon sugar

2 cups all-purpose flour, plus a little extra for rolling

Pinch of salt

4 cups canola or other neutral-flavored oil

3 cups sugar

2 cups whole milk

¼ cup light corn syrup

1 small stick *canela*

¼ teaspoon baking soda

Pinch of salt

⅓ cup unsalted butter

1 teaspoon pure vanilla extract

These delicious candies are made with milk and sugar that is slowly and patiently cooked (most often in heavy copper pots). There are several variations as well, two of which are below.

During my travels in Mexico, I never met any candy makers who used a thermometer because they rely on knowledge, feeling, and instinct, but if you have one I suggest you use it (see page 13) and slowly train your eye. When the recipe asks you to beat the mixture at the end, do not use the spoon you have been stirring with, because any leftover sugar will cause the mixture to rapidly crystallize (if for some reason this happens, though, it makes a delicious ice cream topping).

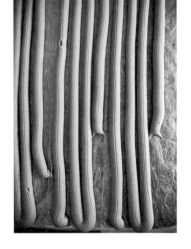

In a tall, heavy pot (at least 5 quarts), combine the sugar, milk, corn syrup, *canela*, baking soda, salt, and butter and bring to a boil, stirring. Cover with a lid for 2 minutes to remove the sugar crystals and cook, stirring occasionally so it doesn't scorch the bottom of the pan, until it reaches the soft-ball stage, or 235° to 240°F, 20 to 25 minutes.

Remove from the heat, discard the *canela*, and let cool for 30 minutes until it is about 180°F. Meanwhile, grease an 8 by 8-inch pan, line it with parchment paper, and butter it again.

When the mixture has cooled, add the vanilla and beat by hand with a clean wooden spoon until the mixture thickens and loses its gloss, about 5 minutes. Pour the mixture into the prepared pan and smooth it out with an offset or a rubber spatula. Allow to set, about 6 hours, and cut into 1- by 2-inch rectangles. Alternatively, you can put the mixture into a piping bag with a starred tip and pipe into 4-inch logs over wax or parchment paper and allow to cool.

MAKES ABOUT 4 DOZEN

VARIATION: MARINAS

Form the mixture into Ping-Pong-size balls and lightly flatten with the palm of your hand. Place on wax or parchment paper, put a toasted pecan half in the center of each, and press down gently; allow to cool.

CONTINUED

VARIATION: MORELIANAS
_____

Preheat the oven to 400°F. Form the mixture into Ping-Pong-size balls and flatten between two heavy pieces of plastic using a tortilla press or rolling pin so they are about ¹⁄₁₆ inch thick (like a tortilla), then transfer to a heavily greased baking sheet. Bake until the tops are browned, 5 to 7 minutes. Let cool. If you are going to store them, put pieces of wax or parchment paper between the layers.

Nogada de Nuez | Piloncillo Candied Pecans
_____

Chihuahua, a state in the north of Mexico, is filled with *nogales*, the pecan tree that adorns many of the valleys and towns in the area, and there are hundreds of dishes and desserts where the pecan is the featured star. One of my favorite pecan recipes is this one prepared by Marisela Chavez de Romo, a very kind and sweet woman who opened her home to me and showed me the proper way to select and clean pecans during an afternoon of pecan-based recipes. These wonderful treats are special because of their unexpected molassy flavor.

8 ounces *piloncillo*, finely chopped

1 (1-inch) piece *canela*

¹⁄₃ cup water

15 ounces unsalted raw pecan halves

Combine the *piloncillo*, *canela*, and water in a pan over medium heat and cook until melted and bubbling heavily, 4 to 6 minutes. The mixture should look thick and golden. Add one-third of the pecans and stir to coat. Add the remaining pecans in two more batches, stirring constantly. The *piloncillo* will begin to crystallize and look sandy, 3 to 5 minutes. This is what we want. Continue stirring until all the pecans are coated.

Pour onto a lightly greased baking sheet, separate with your hands or a spoon, and let cool completely. Store in an airtight container in a cool, dry area for up to 3 weeks.

MAKES 2 QUARTS

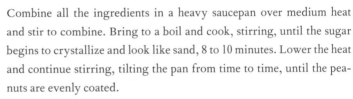

2 cups unsalted raw peanuts
(preferably with red skins)

1 cup sugar

½ cup water

¼ teaspoon salt

I have not been able to have these for a very long time because I became allergic to peanuts about fifteen years ago, but I always looked for them on my way to the movies when I was little. It was one of my favorite treats—a long tube of soft plastic, filled with crunchy, sweet red balls that never lasted through the movie. I never realized or even questioned how they were made, but I definitely remember being fascinated by the idea that each peanut was encapsulated in a sugary, crunchy coating.

I have not put any food coloring in these because I prefer the caramel color, and I don't think the traditional red adds anything to the recipe. I am certain you will end up making these again and again.

Combine all the ingredients in a heavy saucepan over medium heat and stir to combine. Bring to a boil and cook, stirring, until the sugar begins to crystallize and look like sand, 8 to 10 minutes. Lower the heat and continue stirring, tilting the pan from time to time, until the peanuts are evenly coated.

Pour onto a lightly greased baking sheet and let sit until cool enough to handle. Separate the clumped peanuts with your hands or two spoons. Store in an airtight container in a cool, dry area for up to 3 weeks.

MAKES ABOUT 2¼ CUPS

Besitos de Nuez | Pecan "Kisses"

One of my favorite candy stores in Puebla is called El Lirio. The owner of the store, Sara Martinez Muñoz, is a lovely woman with white hair and a fighting spirit, who loves to play jokes on her customers. She says that when she sees couples entering the store unsure of what to get, she quietly asks the woman to give her partner a little kiss (which is the name of the candy). Most hesitate, but then oblige—how could they refuse a nice old lady? As they approach the counter, she slowly walks with her cane toward the edge of it, and as the man bends over, she hands him a *besito*. Invariably they laugh and blush, but it is all soon forgotten once they take a bite of this delicacy. She says the name comes from the fact that they are small and delicious and leave you wanting more, the way a real kiss does.

Finely grind the pecans in a food processor, making sure you don't form a paste. Put the sugar and water in a heavy pot and bring to a boil over medium heat. Add the ground pecans and stir constantly until thickened, 5 to 10 minutes. Transfer to a food processor and grind into a smooth paste.

Roll into small marble-size balls with dampened hands or a small scoop (dip in warm water as needed, removing the excess). Roll in sugar to coat and serve as is or in small paper liners.

MAKES ABOUT 4 DOZEN

3 cups pecans, toasted

1 cup sugar, plus extra for rolling

½ cup water

1 cup heavy cream

5 tablespoons unsalted butter

4 teaspoons salt

1½ cups sugar

¼ cup light corn syrup

⅓ cup water

1 cup unsalted pistachios, lightly toasted and coarsely chopped

One of my mom's friends, Yoya, gave me this family recipe long ago and I absolutely love it. Because you caramelize the sugar early in the process, the time it takes to prepare the caramel is much shorter than with other recipes. These make wonderful gifts and are nice to have around for guests.

Lightly butter the bottom and sides of an 8-inch square pan. Cover with parchment paper or aluminum foil (the butter will help it adhere to the pan). Butter the parchment or foil and set aside.

Place the cream, butter, and salt in a small saucepan over medium heat and bring to a boil. Remove from the heat and set aside.

Place the sugar, corn syrup, and water in a heavy, deep saucepan or pot over medium heat and cook, stirring, until the sugar is dissolved. Continue cooking until the mixture starts to turn golden, then swirl lightly to caramelize evenly.

Remove from the heat and whisk in the cream mixture, being very careful because it will bubble up and steam. Once it stops bubbling, return the mixture to the heat and continue to cook, adjusting the heat to maintain a constant soft simmer, until it reaches 248°F on a candy thermometer, about 15 minutes. Stir in the pistachios and pour into the prepared pan.

Let sit for 2 to 3 hours, until cool to the touch. Cut into 1-inch pieces and wrap each piece in a piece of cellophane or wax paper, twisting the ends to secure. Store in an airtight container in a cool, dry place for about 1 month.

MAKES 64

Precision in Candy Making

The *punto,* the exact moment when the candy is ready varies not only between different types of candy but also with relation to personal preference. It is one of the most important aspects of the candy making process because it defines the texture. Throughout my travels, whenever I asked someone when they'd know their creation was ready, they always responded "when it reaches the *punto.*" I didn't find one person in Mexico who relied on thermometers or cared to have one. They rely on their senses and experience and are artisans in the truest sense of the word.

Glorias | Pecan Fudge Caramels

If you've visited Mexico, you've probably tried these goat's milk caramel candies mixed with pecans and wrapped in bright red cellophane paper. The name *gloria* means "glorious," and that's exactly what these confections are. There are many versions of this candy made primarily in Linares, a city located in the south of Nuevo Leon. This recipe requires patience and a candy thermometer, but it isn't difficult and the candies make very nice gifts.

2 cups whole goat's milk

1¼ cups sugar

2 tablespoons light corn syrup

Pinch of salt

¼ teaspoon baking soda

2 teaspoons pure vanilla extract

1 cup finely chopped toasted pecans

Butter a medium baking dish or bowl.

Combine 1 cup of the milk, the sugar, corn syrup, salt, and baking soda in a tall, heavy pot (this is because the milk may rise substantially and can boil over) and cook over medium heat, stirring, until it comes to a boil, and then clip a candy thermometer onto the pot. Lower the heat and cook, stirring, until the mixture reaches 242°F, or is a light caramel color and a lot of the foam has gone away, 25 to 30 minutes.

Slowly, pour the remaining 1 cup milk into the pot and cook until the mixture reaches 246°F. Remove from the heat and stir in the vanilla and pecans. When you stir, some of the sugar will recrystallize, which is what we want so some parts are soft and others are slightly dry. Let sit until it's just cool enough to handle, then scoop into ovals and wrap in red cellophane paper, twisting the ends.

MAKES ABOUT 3 DOZEN

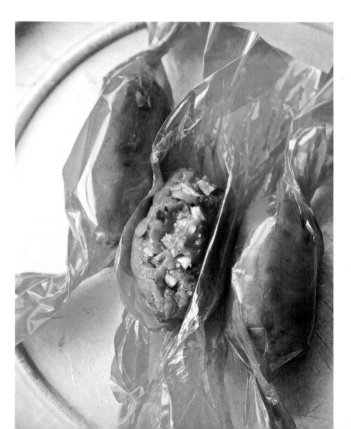

Alfajor de Miel con Nueces y Especias | Honey-Nut Spiced Arab Candy

2 cups honey

1¼ cups ground almonds

1¼ cups ground hazelnuts

1½ cups bread crumbs

¼ cup toasted sesame seeds

1 teaspoon freshly ground *canela*

Pinch of ground cloves

½ teaspoon toasted coriander seeds, ground

½ teaspoon toasted aniseed, ground

16 to 20 rice wafers

There is a really interesting publication from 1969 titled *El Dulce en Mexico* (*The Sweets of Mexico*). One of the things it talks about is old cookbooks with *alfajor* or *alajú* recipes (*alajú* means "the stuffing" in Arabic). The author describes a candy that he called a "type of fruit cake," (even though it doesn't seem to have to do anything with one) from 1786, which I, in turn, have translated. It is basically a sweet paste made from honey and different nuts, which is thinly "sandwiched" between two wafers. They are absolutely addictive! Feel free to play around with different nuts and spice combinations.

Heat the honey in a medium pot over low heat until smooth, 3 to 5 minutes. Add 1 cup of the almonds, 1 cup of the hazelnuts, and the bread crumbs and stir to combine. Once the mixture starts coming together, add the sesame seeds, *canela*, cloves, coriander, and aniseed and stir for a couple of minutes until well blended. Pour into a bowl and let sit until cool enough to handle.

Put a bit of the mixture on top of a rice wafer, spreading it around evenly, and press with your hands to about ¼-inch thickness (you can dampen your hands slightly if the mixture is too sticky). Sprinkle some of the remaining ¼ cup almonds and remaining ¼ cup hazelnuts on top, pressing lightly, then put another wafer on top and press so it sticks.

These are best eaten a day or two later. You can store them in an airtight container in a cool, dry area. Serve whole or cut into quarters.

MAKES 8 TO 10

PAN DULCE

—

MORNING SWEET BREADS

PANADERÍAS (BREAD BAKERIES) ARE FOUND all over Mexico, representing one of the main pillars of Mexican cuisine. Small villages have their *panaderías* close to the main square, like a church. In bygone days, *panaderías* were owned by the Spanish, who were always identified by their berets and cigars. They were the ones who taught Mexicans the secrets of the ovens, which were fueled by coal or wood.

When the *panadería* opens its doors, a familiar, comforting aroma envelops you. After a quick glimpse at the crispy textures and colorful toppings, you pick up a round aluminum tray and a set of banged-up metal tongs, and fill the tray with shapes of ears, flowers, shells, horns, and hearts. Each one contains its own particular taste experience. Once you solve the dilemma of what to take home, you proceed to the counter, where someone will rapidly and skillfully put the pastries in a paper bag and staple it, handing you a small, often handwritten, ticket. You pay and hurry outside. Gluttony can't wait as you open the bag, or rather rip it, take a bite of whatever's on top, and end up eating the whole thing!

But there are other ways to get your *pan dulce* fix. There are markets, men and women with carts who sell them on the streets, and homes with a small storefront or back entrance where shelves surrounding the worktable are filled with freshly baked goods. There is the *canastero* balancing a large handwoven *canasta* (basket) of bread on his head, wiggling down streets on a bicycle and distributing them to construction workers and others.

Some *panaderos* use fresh yeast; others use dry. Some use *pulque* (a fermented beverage made from maguey nectar) or beer. The skillful *panaderos* begin their day at around 3:00 A.M., first making the wonderful morning pastries, which may include cookies and sliced cakes, and then slowly expanding their offerings. Bread is the cornerstone of a good breakfast and is usually accompanied by hot chocolate or coffee. *Panaderías* bake twice daily as a general rule, ensuring warm, fresh baked goods for breakfast, *merienda* (supper), and dinner.

The bread itself is only slightly sweetened. Most of its sweetness comes from fillings, toppings, and glazes. These are made from fruit, sugar, chocolate, and cream. Most *panaderías* have *bolillos* and *teleras*, savory breads that are used to make *tortas*, but the majority of the selections are sweet ones.

In the beginning of the twentieth century, *pan dulce* became affordable to poor people, who called it *tecuarín*. The bread was salty but with a sweet topping, and many types of bread follow

that format today. The basic ingredients of wheat flour, water, sugar, and salt have remained through time, but others have changed. The traditional lard or butter has been replaced with vegetable shortening, margarine, or oil; the hen, duck, or turkey eggs have been replaced with chicken eggs; the use of *pulque* or beer as a fermenting agent is almost gone; and the use of prepared flours and artificial flavorings has increased as an unfortunate result of industrialization and the economy.

Some places, however, have kept the integrity of the traditional sweet breads. Most Mexicans will say that the ones made in the old-style brick or stone ovens, where the logs are burned hours in advance, have a wonderful distinctive flavor. Although many of these *panaderías* have electric mixers, some seem to be there for decorative purposes—many bakers firmly believe that the hand of the *panadero* is irreplaceable and that the heart you put into your bread cannot be felt through a machine. Some small cities and villages—including Zacatlán in Puebla and Pomuch, Campeche, and Acámbaro in Guanajuato—depend on bread as their main source of income. For these *panaderos*, bread is serious business.

As with other sweet confections, each region has its own specialty when it comes to *pan dulce*. *Pan ranchero*, country-style bread often flavored with aniseed, is made in Zacatecas; corn *pemoles* in Aguascalientes; *coyotitas*, crunchy corn cookies, in Sonora; and *corrientes*, a porous bread eaten with hot chocolate, in Morelia. Joletepec is known for its *mestizas*, a lightly sweetened bread in the shape of a heart adorned with a braid around the edges. It is said that in the old days, boyfriends would take a *mestiza* to their future in-laws when they asked for their daughter's hand in marriage. The more ornate and intricate the *mestiza,* the greater his wealth.

If you visit San Juan Huactzingo, Tlaxcala, chances are you will leave smelling a bit like wheat and sugar because many homes have their own *calabazeros* (pumpkin-shaped wood-fired ovens). In the town of Calpán, bread is wrapped in white *zapote* leaves to keep it dry and give it a subtle, sweet flavor. Similarly, in Tinguidín, a town in Michoacán, freshly baked bread is wrapped in banana leaves before it is transported from the different *panaderías*.

Members of the *purépecha* indigenous community make breads in the shapes of animals and people adorned with belts and bows for their offerings in certain celebrations, while the Tepehuas of Tenango de Doria make necklaces out of bread and marigolds for their flower dance. And weddings, baptisms, and offerings have their distinctive breads depending on the region. Mexican culture even conjures death through bread, the symbol of life.

Many of these recipes require a bit of planning, so be sure to take this into account. I have tried to go back to *pan dulce's* roots, when, as I can only imagine, bread was richer. Although I personally like to use fresh yeast instead of dry, I believe it is mostly for the sake of tradition; using dry active yeast will not terribly affect the end product. Finally, most *panaderos* will say that you must knead by hand, but perhaps you should leave that for the experts, unless you want to get a workout!

Rosquillas de Naranja | Orange-Infused Rounds

2 cups all-purpose flour, plus a little extra for rolling

1½ tablespoons baking powder

9 tablespoons unsalted butter, at room temperature

1½ cups sugar

3 eggs, separated

1 tablespoon grated orange zest

½ cup sugar plus 1 teaspoon freshly ground *canela*

Any kind of round cookie with a hole in the middle is called a *rosquilla*. Esther Villarreal Garza from Monterrey makes these sugary ones with a lovely orange flavor.

In a large bowl, combine the flour and baking powder. Beat the butter with a wooden spoon or in a mixer using the paddle attachment for a couple of minutes. Add the sugar and beat until light and fluffy. Add the egg yolks one at a time, then add the orange zest. Scrape down the sides of the bowl and beat until thoroughly combined. Gradually add the flour mixture and beat until incorporated. Knead on a lightly floured surface until a smooth and uniform dough is formed, 3 to 5 minutes.

Using your hands, roll out pieces about 5 inches long and ½ inch thick, starting in the center and rolling outward so that the pieces are evenly thick. Connect one end of each piece to the other, making a ring, and place on a parchment paper–lined baking sheet at least 1 inch apart (they will spread a little). Refrigerate until firm to the touch, 10 minutes or so.

Meanwhile, preheat the oven to 350°F.

Beat the egg whites lightly with a fork, brush the tops of the *rosquillas*, and carefully dip the tops into the cinnamon-sugar mixture. Bake until they are lightly golden around the edges, 10 to 15 minutes, and transfer to a wire rack to cool. These are best the day they are made.

MAKES 2½ TO 3 DOZEN

Conchas Blancas | White Shells

Ah, the *conchas*! These wonderful soft breads with their crunchy shell-like topping are a favorite in Mexico. This particular recipe is based on one made by Irving Quiros, a pastry instructor at the Colegio Superior de Gastronomía in Puebla. The dough is almost like a brioche, and the buttery bun makes wonderful, melt-in-your-mouth *conchas*. To make a chocolate topping, substitute 3 tablespoons cocoa powder for 3 tablespoons flour.

TO MAKE THE DOUGH, dissolve the yeast in the milk. Separately, combine 4 cups of the bread flour with the granulated sugar in a mixer with the hook attachment. Add the dissolved yeast and mix lightly. Add the salt and the eggs, one at a time, while mixing on low speed until the mixture starts to come together. Scrape the sides, increase the speed to medium, and continue to mix until a smooth and elastic dough forms, about 10 minutes. Add the butter little by little, increase the speed to medium-high, and mix until the dough looks smooth and shiny but doesn't tear when you stretch it lightly, 8 to 10 minutes. If it is too sticky, add the remaining ½ cup flour, little by little, and avoid the temptation to add too much.

Lightly oil a large bowl and place the dough inside. Cover with a slightly damp towel or plastic wrap and let sit in a warm place (about 70°F) until doubled in size, 60 to 80 minutes. Gather the edges together and flip over so that the bottom is now the top, and cover with plastic wrap. Refrigerate overnight (chilling it will slow the fermentation process and the dough will be easier to shape).

Remove the dough from the refrigerator, uncover, and place a towel on top. Leave the dough to rise in a warm place (about 70°F) to come to room temperature, about 1 hour. Meanwhile, prepare the topping.

TO MAKE THE TOPPING, combine the all-purpose flour, baking powder, salt, and confectioner's sugar in a large bowl. (If using cocoa powder, add it now.) Cream the butter in a separate bowl, add the flour mixture, and mix until well combined. Add the vanilla and mix well.

Divide the dough into 2-ounce pieces (about the size of a tennis ball) and roll tightly by cupping your hands and pressing as you roll it over the table (use only a little flour if it starts to stick). Place on a parchment paper–lined baking sheet about 1 inch apart and press down with the palm of your hand so it looks like a dome.

Roll a gumball-size amount of topping in your hands and flatten it so that it covers the dome of dough. Score with the tip of a sharp paring knife to make parallel curved lines to resemble a seashell. Let sit

Dough

1 tablespoon plus 2 teaspoons active dry yeast

1¼ cups whole milk, at room temperature

4 to 4½ cups bread flour

¾ cup granulated sugar

2 teaspoons salt

3 eggs

1 cup unsalted butter, at room temperature

Topping

2 cups all-purpose flour

½ teaspoon baking powder

Pinch of salt

2 cups confectioner's sugar

½ cup unsalted butter, at room temperature

½ teaspoon pure vanilla extract or ½ teaspoon freshly ground *canela* (depending on personal preference)

at room temperature until doubled in size and the dough springs back when pressed lightly on the side, 35 to 45 minutes.

Preheat the oven to 350°F.

Bake the *conchas* until the bottoms and sides are golden, 30 to 40 minutes. Allow to cool, if you can resist.

MAKES 18

Garibaldis | Buttery Muffins with Apricot Jam and Sprinkles

1⅓ cups all-purpose flour

1¼ teaspoons baking powder

Pinch of salt

¾ cup unsalted butter, at room temperature

¾ cup sugar

2 eggs, at room temperature

½ teaspoon pure vanilla extract

½ cup whole milk

1 cup apricot jam

1 to 2 cups white sprinkles (the kind that looks like dots, not stripes)

You know how people love to eat muffin tops? Well, these muffins have a topping on the sides as well. Whenever we bought them, my mom would always take a bit off the top, then the sides, and leave the center in the tray as if it was the most natural thing to do! Their flavor is deliciously subtle and they are a favorite among my whole family.

Preheat the oven to 350°F. Butter and flour a standard muffin tin.

Combine the flour, baking powder, and salt in a large bowl. In a separate bowl, cream the butter with the sugar until pale and fluffy. In a third bowl, combine the eggs, vanilla, and milk and add to the butter mixture in three additions, alternating with the flour mixture, scraping the sides as needed.

Pour the batter into the muffin cups, filling them three-fourths full, and bake until a toothpick inserted into the center comes out clean and the muffins spring back when touched in the center, 15 to 20 minutes.

Remove from the oven, let cool for about 10 minutes, and turn out onto a wire rack to cool completely.

If the jam is too thick and sticky to spread without tearing the muffins, heat it slightly in a small pan over medium-low heat or in the microwave. Spread around the sides and tops of the muffins and roll in the sprinkles.

MAKES 1 DOZEN

3 cups water

2 long sticks *canela*,
broken into pieces

¼ teaspoon salt

½ cup unsalted butter

2 cups all-purpose flour

4 ounces *queso fresco*, crumbled

2 eggs

Vegetable oil, for frying

½ cup sugar plus 1 teaspoon
freshly ground *canela*, for rolling

It is a spectacle to see these fritters made at the *churreria* that opened in 1935, called Los Churros del Moro, in downtown Mexico City. The *churro* master, as I call him, presses a lever that pushes out the soft dough, and as it hits the oil, he moves it, forming a large coil that looks like a six-foot-long snake all curled up. He very gently bathes it with the oil. When it is golden, he pulls it out and drains it on a round metal tray. It is then handed to another *churro* master, who cuts it with scissors into long strips the size of a straw and rolls the strips in plain sugar or a ground *canela*–sugar mixture. You can get hot chocolate (there are five types: *Vienna, Francesca, Español, Especial,* and *Mexicano,* varying in sweetness) to accompany them, although some people prefer to dip them in warm *cajeta* or chocolate sauce. I knew the famed *churreria* was not going to share its recipe (I have tried for a long time), so I was always on the lookout for one that was close enough . . .

Then one day, while visiting the Mercado Pino Suarez (the main market) in Villa Hermosa, Tabasco, I was suddenly distracted by the distinctive aroma of freshly made *churros.* I followed the scent, which led me to a small corner stand. The *churros* were warm, a little puffier than those at del Moro, and absolutely, undoubtedly, one of the best I'd ever had. There was no hot chocolate or sauce to dip them into. Just pure crunchy, sweet fritters with an intense cinnamon flavor and a little something else I couldn't quite make out. I really wanted the recipe, and after a little talking and smiling, I was allowed to visit the next day to see how they were made. So, there I was, walking alone on the streets of this not-so-safe place, at 4:00 in the morning. It was still dark, and there were a few people around: some were just finishing their night and others were busy getting ready to open their businesses. I am not a morning person at all, but making *churros* at a market in Mexico is definitely an antidote to morning crankiness. The secret ingredient in these *churros*? *Queso fresco*!

Here is the adapted recipe from Lorenzo Sanches Mendoza from the stand El As Negro, with my profound thanks.

Combine the water and *canela* sticks in a medium pot and cook over medium heat until reduced to 2 cups, 15 to 20 minutes. Strain through a fine-mesh sieve and discard the *canela*. Place back in the pot, add the salt and butter, and cook over medium heat until melted. Remove from the heat and add the flour all at once, stirring vigorously to remove any

CONTINUED

lumps. Continue stirring until the dough comes together into a smooth ball. Allow the mixture to cool in the pan for 5 to 10 minutes, and then add the *queso fresco*, stirring to incorporate. Add the eggs, one at a time, and stir until the dough is nice and smooth.

Pour the oil into a large, deep pan or skillet to a depth of at least 2 inches and heat over high heat to 350°F. (To test the temperature, drop a bit of dough into the oil. It should sink and quickly float to the top and bubble.)

Put some of the dough into a *churrera* or a heavy canvas bag fitted with a star tip. (A closed-star tip is best for creating the deep ridges associated with churros.) Squeeze or press out long strips (5 to 6 inches) of dough directly over the oil and cut off the ends with scissors. Fry a few at a time, turning so that they are evenly golden on all sides, 4 to 6 minutes. (Caution: Air pockets that form in the dough as you press it out and a frying oil that's not hot enough will make the *churros* burst.) Remove with a slotted spoon and drain on paper bags or towels. Let cool slightly so you can make sure they are cooked through (they should be soft inside and an even color, with no traces of raw dough). Roll in the *canela*-sugar mixture while still warm so that the mixture sticks to them. Eat warm with some frothy hot Mexican chocolate.

MAKES ABOUT 20

1 recipe Empanada dough
(page 133)

Filling

2 cups *requesón* (about 20 ounces)

½ cup sugar, plus more
for sprinkling

½ cup sour cream

¼ cup all-purpose flour

Grated zest of 1 lime

1 teaspoon pure vanilla extract

2 eggs

1 egg yolk mixed with
1 tablespoon whole milk or
cream, for egg wash

Requesón is a slightly grainy, lightly salted cheese somewhere between ricotta and pot cheese. Lime zest complements the cheese filling hidden inside the golden, flaky crust. These are a really nice option for a brunch menu, and if you make the dough ahead of time, you can make these in a jiffy!

Lightly grease a standard-size muffin tin. Line a baking sheet with parchment paper.

On a lightly floured surface, roll about two-thirds of the dough to ⅛ inch thickness. With a cookie cutter or large glass, cut out 12 circles about 3¾ inches in diameter and press into the bottom and up the sides of the muffin cups. The dough may crack or break, but just press it together with your fingers. Make sure they are about the same thickness all around. Reroll the scraps and the remaining one-third dough to the same thickness and cut out 12 circles that are the same size as the tops of the muffin cups. Place the cups and the tops on the prepared baking sheet and refrigerate while you prepare the filling (the dough can be made up to 3 days ahead of time but needs to be taken out and allowed to come to room temperature before unwrapping and using).

Preheat the oven to 350°F.

TO MAKE THE FILLING, place the cheese in a cheesecloth-lined bowl and drain the excess liquid. Combine the drained cheese, the sugar, sour cream, flour, lime zest, vanilla, and eggs in a blender or food processor and blend until smooth.

Remove the chilled dough from the refrigerator. Spoon the cheese filling into the dough cups almost to the top. Lightly wet the edges of the dough cups with your fingers and place 1 dough circle on top of each cup. Press lightly to seal the edges. Brush the tops with the egg wash and sprinkle with the sugar. Bake until golden brown, 25 to 30 minutes. Let cool for a few minutes in the pan, then carefully flip the pan to unmold the pies and let cool on a wire rack.

MAKES 1 DOZEN

Campechanas | Sugary Flaky Pastries

Campechanas are fragile, crunchy, glasslike sweet treats that crumble as you take a bite. Valle de Bravo, a town a few hours from Mexico City, has some of the best ones, but you can find them everywhere. Funnily enough, though, they are hard to find in Campeche, where their name comes from.

They are a bit tricky to make, but once you start, you'll quickly get the hang of it. You may be surprised by the amount of fat that goes into these, especially because you couldn't tell from eating them. The lard or shortening is what makes these incredibly flaky. You will need a very thin rolling pin that is at least 15 inches long and no thicker than the stick of a broom; you can find one at a hardware store or a woodshop.

14 ounces lard or vegetable shortening, at room temperature

4½ cups all-purpose flour

Pinch of salt

1 to 1⅜ cups sugar

1¼ cups tepid water

½ cup unsalted butter, at room temperature

Beat 2 ounces of the lard with 3½ cups of the flour, the salt, and 2 tablespoons of the sugar in a mixer with a hook attachment until almost fully combined. Gradually add the water and continue to mix on medium speed until the mixture comes off the sides of the bowl and is smooth, 10 to 15 minutes. Divide the dough in half, cutting it with a bench scraper or knife but not tearing it, roll it lightly, and smear the tops with some of the remaining lard using your hands. Allow it to rest for 10 minutes.

In a bowl, combine 4 ounces of the remaining lard with the butter and the remaining 1 cup flour and stir with a wooden spoon or spatula until well combined. Set aside.

Grease a work surface with some of the remaining 8 ounces lard and flatten one of the halves of the dough with your hands into a rectangle. Grease a thin rolling pin (see headnote) and roll the dough as thin as possible, without tearing, into a rectangle about 12 inches wide by 4 inches long. Turn the dough so the width is closest to you.

Smear half of the reserved flour-fat mixture evenly on top of the rolled-out dough. Grease the rolling pin with a little more lard and roll the dough tightly but carefully onto the rolling pin. Make sure your hands are greased (use a bit more lard if you need to). Grab an end of the rolling pin with one hand and pull the dough out with the other. You will now have a dough that looks a bit like a snake. Stretch it out to the sides so that the roll is about 25 inches long and about ½ inch thick. Flatten the dough by lightly pressing it with your hands or the rolling pin and cut into twelve 4-inch pieces. Place on a baking sheet (no need to line it or grease it), and lightly flatten the rectangles with your hands so they are a bit like ovals. Repeat with the remaining half of the dough and the remaining half of the flour-fat mixture.

Preheat the oven to 375°F.

Set the racks in the top half of the oven, smear a bit more of the remaining lard on top, and liberally sprinkle with the remaining 1 to 1¼ cups sugar (don't be shy). Tap any excess sugar from the baking sheets by tilting them, then bake, turning the sheets halfway through so they bake evenly (or bake them one at a time), until the pastries are puffed and slightly brown, 15 to 20 minutes. Increase the temperature to 425°F and continue baking, watching closely, until the tops are shiny and golden, about 5 minutes. Allow to cool before eating.

MAKES 1 TO 1½ DOZEN

Rosca de Reyes | Three Kings Bread

Bread

1 recipe Pan de Muerto dough (page 109), chilled overnight

4 to 6 plastic baby figurines

3 ounces assorted candied fruits (such as orange, fig, *acitrón*, and lime)

1 egg, beaten

Topping

⅓ cup all-purpose flour

⅓ cup sugar, plus more for sprinkling (about ¼ cup)

6 tablespoons butter or vegetable shortening, at room temperature

½ teaspoon pure vanilla extract

Three kings bread is a very tasty and colorfully decorated bread adorned with candied fruit and a sugary topping and with a tiny plastic figurine baked into it.

In Mexico, this bread brings friends and families together for the annual Three Kings celebration on the January 6. It is one of the most important festivities because it represents the day Jesus became known to the world. The Church recognizes it as one of the most important celebrations. This particular bread was brought by the Spaniards as one of the religious traditions that they instilled in the pre-Hispanic lands. Traditionally, the bread was round, but it is most often oval nowadays.

In the old days, a candy or fava bean was hidden inside. It is believed that this was a representation of people wanting to hide and protect Jesus. Unfortunately, many people swallowed them by mistake, so the tradition changed to have a figurine inside. The first ones were made out of plaster or porcelain; but now, plastic figurines are used.

The nativity scene is supposed to be removed on January 6, and those who find the figurine (baby Jesus) become a sort of guardian who will take care of him until February 2, when they dress him up for the Candlemas celebration. It is a day of feasting, and those who got the figurines must treat all those whom they shared the bread with to a traditional fiesta of tamales and *atole*.

CONTINUED

TO MAKE THE BREAD, bring the chilled dough to room temperature, still covered, about 1 hour. Divide the dough in half by cutting, not pulling, it and roll each one tightly into a ball, cupping your hands and pressing as you roll it over the table. Poke a hole in the center of each ball and carefully stretch it into a large donut. Carefully tuck the figurines into the dough from the bottom (using 2 to 3 per bread), pressing each figurine in and smoothing the dough over so it's completely hidden. Place the dough on a parchment paper–lined baking sheet and cover lightly with a cloth. Let rise until doubled, about 1 hour, but preheat the oven to 350°F after about 40 minutes.

Cut the candied fruit into strips or desired shapes. Brush the beaten egg all over the top of the dough. Decorate with the candied fruit, leaving some space for the crunchy topping.

TO MAKE THE TOPPING, combine the flour, sugar, and butter in a large bowl and mix until well combined. Add the vanilla and mix well. You should have a smooth and malleable dough, but if it's a bit sticky simply add a little flour. Roll into gumball-size balls with your hands and press lightly between your palms so you have an oval shape. Lightly press into the spaces on the top of the dough. Sprinkle with some sugar and bake until the bottoms are golden, 40 to 50 minutes.

MAKES 2

Huachibolas | Cream Cheese Morning Rolls

The small bicycle town of Pomuch in Campeche has some of the best bakeries in Mexico. One of the oldest, La Huachita, still uses a brick oven and has been around for 120 years. They were kind enough to let me spend hours as a spectator, and this is a recipe I adapted from one of their creations. These small sugary breads are slightly flaky, buttery, and filled with a rich cream cheese mixture.

TO MAKE THE DOUGH, dissolve the yeast in the water, add ¼ cup of the flour, stir to combine, and leave in a warm place (about 70°F) until it begins to bubble and puffs up slightly, 20 to 30 minutes.

Put 2¾ cups of the remaining flour in the bowl of a mixer fitted with the hook attachment, add the granulated sugar and salt, and mix

Dough

2¼ teaspoons active dry yeast

½ cup tepid water

3 to 3½ cups bread flour, sifted

⅓ cup granulated sugar

½ teaspoon salt

3 eggs, at room temperature

¼ cup unsalted butter, at room temperature

Filling

8 ounces cream cheese,
at room temperature

3 tablespoons
confectioner's sugar

Pinch of salt

1 egg , lightly beaten

Granulated sugar, for sprinkling

for about 30 seconds. Add the eggs and the yeast dough. Mix at low speed until the dough starts to come together. Add the butter gradually, in small pieces, while continuing to mix, and increase the speed to medium-high. The dough will look sticky, but resist the temptation to add more flour. Continue beating until the dough is soft and comes off the sides of the bowl, about 10 minutes. If the dough is still sticky after 10 minutes of beating, you may now add a little of the remaining ½ cup flour until it no longer sticks to the sides.

Lightly grease a large bowl with oil or and place the dough inside. Cover with a towel and let rise in a warm place (about 70°F) until doubled in size, about 1½ hours. Punch down gently, gather the sides together, flip over so that the bottom is now the top, and cover with plastic wrap. Refrigerate for at least 4 hours or overnight (chilling it will slow the fermentation process, making it easier to shape). Remove the dough from the refrigerator, uncover, and place a towel on top. Leave the dough to rise in a warm place (about 70°F) to come to room temperature, about 1 hour.

TO MAKE THE FILLING, beat the cream cheese with the confectioner's sugar and salt using the paddle attachment of a mixer or by hand. Roll out the dough to about ½ inch thick and cut into 4-inch squares (you should have about 18). Spoon about 1 tablespoon of the cream cheese filling in the center of each square and bring all the edges toward the middle. Press so that they stick together, turn over, and carefully tighten into rounds on a lightly floured surface. Cover with a towel and let rise in a warm place (about 70°F) until doubled in size, about 45 minutes. To tell whether the dough has doubled, press lightly with your finger. It should slowly spring all the way back.

Preheat the oven to 375°F.

Brush the tops of the pastries with the beaten egg. Generously sprinkle with granulated sugar and bake until the tops are golden, 25 to 35 minutes. Transfer to a wire rack, and let cool.

MAKES ABOUT 18

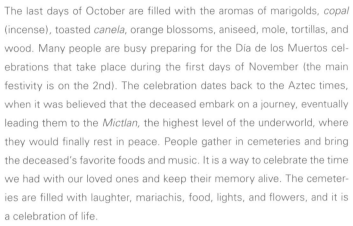

Dough

2¼ teaspoons active dry yeast

2 tablespoons orange blossom water

⅔ cup whole milk

4 cups bread flour

½ cup sugar

1 teaspoon salt

1 teaspoon grated orange zest

4 eggs, lightly beaten

1 cup unsalted butter, at room temperature

Topping

¼ cup unsalted butter

½ cup sugar

The last days of October are filled with the aromas of marigolds, *copal* (incense), toasted *canela*, orange blossoms, aniseed, mole, tortillas, and wood. Many people are busy preparing for the Día de los Muertos celebrations that take place during the first days of November (the main festivity is on the 2nd). The celebration dates back to the Aztec times, when it was believed that the deceased embark on a journey, eventually leading them to the *Mictlan,* the highest level of the underworld, where they would finally rest in peace. People gather in cemeteries and bring the deceased's favorite foods and music. It is a way to celebrate the time we had with our loved ones and keep their memory alive. The cemeteries are filled with laughter, mariachis, food, lights, and flowers, and it is a celebration of life.

There are many different breads made for this celebration. In Michoacán, they are sculpted into shapes of flowers, the Virgin Mary, skulls, and animals. In Oaxaca, you will find round breads topped with sesame seeds and colorful heads coming out of them. In the center of Mexico, the dough is made with *pulque* (a fermented beverage made from the maguey plant) instead of yeast, giving it a very distinctive, somewhat herbal, acidic flavor. Many places dust the tops with pink sugar to remind us of the ceremonial use of bread. The varieties are too many to count, but this one is perhaps the most well known. This recipe is adapted from Maricu, a chef from Mexico City who owns a cooking school of the same name.

Even though you may not celebrate Día de los Muertos, I encourage you to make this delicious bread decorated with "bones" and take a moment to remember those who are no longer with you in this life.

TO MAKE THE DOUGH, dissolve the yeast in the orange blossom water. Add ⅓ cup of the milk and ½ cup of the flour. Mix well with a whisk (the dough should be sticky and smooth) and leave in a warm place (about 70°F) until it begins to bubble and puffs up slightly, 20 to 30 minutes.

Put the remaining 3½ cups flour in the bowl of a mixer with the hook attachment and mix in the sugar, salt, and orange zest for about 30 seconds. Add the eggs, the remaining ⅓ cup milk, and the yeast dough. Mix at low speed until the dough starts to come together. Add the butter gradually, in small pieces, while continuing to mix, and increase the speed to medium. The dough will look sticky, but resist the temptation to add more flour. Continue beating for 10 to 15 minutes, until the dough is soft and comes off the sides of the bowl. If the dough is

CONTINUED

still sticky after 15 minutes of beating, you may now add a little flour, if needed (no more than ⅓ cup).

Lightly grease a large bowl with oil or butter and place the dough inside. Cover with a towel and let rise in a warm place (about 70°F) until doubled in size, 1 to 1½ hours. Punch down the dough, gather the sides together, flip over so that the bottom is now the top, and cover with plastic wrap. Refrigerate for at least 4 hours or overnight (chilling it will slow the fermentation process and make it easier to shape). Remove the dough from the refrigerator, uncover, and place a towel on top. Leave the dough to rise in a warm place (about 70°F) to come to room temperature, about 1 hour.

Cut off (don't pull) a piece of dough about the size of a large lime and reserve to make the "bones." Divide the remaining dough in half and form into 2 rounds, shaping them on a smooth surface and making sure the dough is compact. Place on 2 baking sheets lined with parchment paper or silicone baking mats. Lightly flatten the tops of the dough rounds with the palm of your hand.

Form some of the reserved dough into 2 gumball-size balls and leave on the baking sheet for later use. Divide the remaining dough into 4 pieces. Roll out with your hands from the center out, making strips that are about 1 inch longer than the width of the rounds. Spread your fingers and press lightly, making knobs that resemble bones. Place 2 strips on top of each bread round, crossing the strips over each other. Cover lightly with a cloth. Let rise in a warm place (about 70°F) until doubled in size, about 1½ hours. To tell whether the dough has doubled, press lightly with your finger. It should slowly spring all the way back.

Preheat the oven to 350°F.

Place the small reserved balls in the center of the bread rounds, where the strips meet, using a little water to make them stick. Bake until the dough has an even, dark golden color, 20 to 30 minutes, then cover loosely with foil and bake until the internal temperature is 190°F or the bottom of the bread is browned, 10 to 15 minutes longer. Remove from the oven and allow to cool for a few minutes on a wire rack.

TO MAKE THE TOPPING, melt the butter and brush on the breads, being sure to brush all around the knobs and over every inch. Hold each bread by the bottom (if it's too warm, use gloves or a piece of cardboard to hold it) and sprinkle evenly with sugar all over the top.

MAKES 2, EACH SERVES 6 TO 8

CONTINUED

Pan de Muerto (continued)

VARIATION: ANISEED

Substitute 1½ teaspoons aniseed for the orange zest and 2 tablespoons whole milk for the orange blossom water.

VARIATION: CINNAMON

Substitute 1 tablespoon coarsely ground toasted *canela* for the orange zest and 2 tablespoons whole milk for the orange blossom water. Sprinkle the bread with confectioner's sugar instead of granulated sugar.

VARIATION: SESAME SEED

For a more savory bread, brush the tops with egg yolk and sprinkle with about ½ cup sesame seeds before baking (no butter or sugar is used at the end).

Hebillas | Buckle Morning Pastries

I want to thank Victor Gomar for sharing the recipe for these quick and fun morning pastries that are more like cookies. The sugary cocoa dough in the center helps shape them like a belt buckle and the same dough can be used to make playful worms (*gusanitos*) filled with jam (opposite page), Pastry Cream (page 164), or Cheese Filling (page 103).

TO MAKE THE DOUGH, In a large bowl, combine the flour, baking powder, *canela*, and salt. In a separate bowl, cream together the butter, lard, and sugar until light and fluffy. Add the eggs, one at a time, scraping the sides as needed, and then add the milk and stir to combine. Add the flour mixture gradually and stir until just combined. Turn out onto a lightly floured surface and knead for a few minutes until a uniform dough forms. Cover with plastic wrap.

TO MAKE THE FILLING, combine the sugar, butter, flour, and cocoa powder in a bowl and knead with your hands until uniform and pliable. (You can also prepare this in a mixer with the paddle attachment.)

Dough

2 cups all-purpose flour, plus a little extra for rolling

1 teaspoon baking powder

1 teaspoon freshly ground *canela*

Pinch of salt

2½ tablespoons unsalted butter, at room temperature

3 tablespoons lard, at room temperature

⅓ cup sugar

2 eggs

¼ cup whole milk

Filling

½ cup sugar

7 tablespoons unsalted butter, at room temperature

1 cup all-purpose flour

2 tablespoons unsweetened natural cocoa powder, preferably Dutch processed

Sugar, for sprinkling

Divide the dough into twelve 2-ounce pieces (about the size of a golf ball) and roll out each piece into an oval about ¼ inch thick, using as little flour as possible. Press about 1 tablespoon of the cocoa filling into the center of the dough, flatten with your hands, and pass a rolling pin over it once or twice to spread evenly. Roll the long edges toward the center, leaving the filling exposed, and turn over. Take the two short edges that haven't been rolled and press them together lightly. Turn over and place on a parchment paper–lined baking sheet. Refrigerate while you preheat the oven.

Preheat the oven to 350°F.

Remove the pastries from the refrigerator and bake until starting to turn golden, 10 to 15 minutes. Remove from the oven, allow to cool slightly, then sprinkle sugar on top while still warm.

MAKES ABOUT 1 DOZEN

VARIATION: GUSANITOS

After forming the 12 oval dough shapes, using a small sharp knife, lightly score horizontal lines as close to each other as possible, making sure you don't cut through the dough. Turn over the dough and spoon about 2 teaspoons of jam (strawberry, pineapple, or guava are good options) into the center, making a little line without away from the edges. Fold each side toward the center, overlapping slightly so that they stick. Turn over and place on a parchment paper–lined baking sheet. Continue with the recipe as directed above.

Donas Rellenas de Mermelada de Fresa | Strawberry Jelly Doughnuts

When we were little, my sister Yael and I would often hang out with our aunts Cucus (her real name is Lina, but I don't think we knew that back then) and Alex. They liked to take us to the *parque España,* one of the few parks in Mexico City, and I always made sure to ask my mom whether she needed us to drop off or pick up anything from the dry cleaner, which was only a few blocks away from the park. I was such a good daughter. . . . Truth be told, there was an ulterior motive. Across the street was a wonderful bakery, and I would always get strawberry jelly–filled doughnuts with a sugary topping. Invariably, I would squirt jelly all over myself and get my aunts in trouble, because my mother warned them not to give us sweets too often.

The bakery, unfortunately, no longer exists, but my memory of what those doughnuts tasted like still does—even though the last time I had them was almost two decades ago. They are a bit time-consuming to make but well worth the effort. You can substitute the jam for a store-bought kind, but if you happen to be making these during strawberry season, I highly suggest you give it a try because it is quite easy and absolutely delicious!

TO MAKE THE DOUGH, combine the yeast and ½ cup of the milk in a bowl, stirring until the yeast is dissolved. Let sit until it begins to foam, about 5 minutes.

Combine 4 cups of the flour with the sugar in a mixer with the hook attachment and add the foamy yeast mixture. Scrape the vanilla bean into the mixture and add the remaining ¾ cup milk, the salt, eggs, and egg yolks. Discard the vanilla bean or save for another use. Mix on low speed until the dough starts to come together, and then add the butter. Increase the speed to medium and mix until the dough is smooth and elastic, 15 to 20 minutes. It will be slightly sticky but shouldn't tear easily.

Lightly coat a large bowl with canola or vegetable oil. Put the dough inside and cover with a slightly damp towel or plastic wrap. Let rise in a warm area (about 70°F) until doubled in size, about 1½ hours. Once it's doubled, bring the edges to the center and turn over.

Turn the dough out onto a lightly floured surface. Roll out into a rectangle about ½ inch thick and cut out as many 2½-inch circles as possible. Put them on a parchment paper–lined baking sheet and cover lightly with a towel.

Gather the scraps and put them on top of each other instead of making a big ball. Reroll the dough (if you feel like the dough is shrinking

Dough

2½ tablespoons active dry yeast

1¼ cups whole milk, at room temperature

4 to 4½ cups bread flour

¾ cup sugar

½ vanilla bean, split lengthwise, or 1 teaspoon lime zest (depending on personal preference)

1 teaspoon salt

2 eggs

5 egg yolks

½ cup unsalted butter, at room temperature

Strawberry Jam

2 pounds strawberries, hulled

2 cups sugar

1 tablespoon fresh lemon or lime juice

Pinch of salt

Vegetable oil, for frying

Sugar, for rolling

as you're trying to roll it out, wrap it in plastic and refrigerate for about 10 minutes) and cut out more circles for a total of about 42. Leave a few pieces of dough of the same thickness to test the oil later. Cover with a towel and let rise in a warm area (about 70°F) until doubled in size and the dough springs back when touched, about 30 minutes.

TO MAKE THE STRAWBERRY JAM, slice or coarsely chop the strawberries and put in a small nonreactive pot with the sugar and lemon juice. Cook over medium heat, stirring, until the sugar dissolves. Add the salt and adjust the heat to maintain a constant soft boil and skim off the foam as it forms. Continue cooking until the jam tightly grabs a spoon or sets when you put a little bit on a cold plate, 15 to 25 minutes.

Pour the oil into a heavy pot to a depth of 3 inches and heat to 375°F (use a piece of the dough you set aside to test the oil; it should sink and then quickly rise to the top and bubble). Fry the doughnuts, a few at a time, turning with a slotted spoon, chopsticks, or tongs, until evenly golden on both sides and puffy, 2 to 3 minutes. Drain on a paper bag or towel and roll in sugar while still warm.

Fit a pastry bag with a small flat tip (about ½ inch) and spoon in the strawberry jam. Insert the tip into the side or bottom of each doughnut and fill with jam. Serve immediately.

MAKES ABOUT 3½ DOZEN

Galletas Blancas de Nuez | White Pecan Cookies

It was dark and chilly outside as my friend Claudia Santa Cruz showed me how to make these marvelous crunchy morsels. As the egg whites whipped, her youngest daughter (about eight years old and a natural-born chef) measured the sugar she would later carefully pour.

We moved to the dining room and three generations filled countless trays of the white kisses that would sit in the oven overnight. Claudia's mother took several to her home because they didn't all fit in the oven. I woke up around 5 A.M. to take a peek, and there was evidence that someone else had already been there, so I knew it was okay to take one. I took another, and before I realized it, I'd had a full meringue breakfast in the silent morning.

Preheat the oven to 225°F. Line a baking sheet with parchment paper or grease lightly.

In a large bowl, combine the pecans, flour, baking powder, and salt. Beat the egg whites with the cream of tartar at medium-high speed until they are foamy and start to thicken but have not quite reached soft peaks. Gradually and slowly add the sugar. Continue beating on high speed for a few minutes, until thick and glossy. Add one-fourth of the pecan mixture and fold carefully so that the eggs don't lose their structure and volume. Repeat, incorporating the remaining pecan mixture in three more additions. Using two small spoons or a piping bag fitted with the flat tip attachment, form little mounds on the prepared baking sheet.

Bake for 1 hour, turn off the oven, and leave the cookies in the oven for another hour. Remove from the oven and let cool on a wire rack.

MAKES ABOUT 4 DOZEN

2½ cups finely chopped pecans

⅓ cup all-purpose flour

½ teaspoon baking powder

Pinch of salt

4 egg whites, at room temperature

¼ teaspoon cream of tartar

1 cup superfine sugar

¾ cup sugar

1 teaspoon freshly ground *canela*

1 recipe Quick Puff Pastry
(page 164)

The name of this crunchy, sugary pastry alludes to their shape. You will find enormous ears in Mexican bakeries, but I've made smaller ones, which are perfect to serve for brunch or with coffee. They're traditionally made with puff pastry, but I've used a mock puff recipe so you can make them at home easily, with less guilt (there is much less butter), and still have plenty of flavor and texture. I like to keep the ready made dough in the freezer so I always have them on hand for guests.

Combine the sugar and *canela* in a small bowl and sprinkle about ¼ cup of the mixture on a work surface. Roll out the puff pastry into a rectangle about 10 by 12 inches and sprinkle another ¼ cup of the mixture on top.

Mark the center of the rectangle (parallel to the long side) very lightly with a knife. Roll one of the long sides toward the center as tightly as possible. Repeat with the other side (both sides should touch in the middle) and press lightly so they stick together. Refrigerate for 30 minutes or freeze (wrap them in parchment paper) for later use.

Preheat the oven to 375°F. Line 2 baking sheets with parchment paper or nonstick mats.

Remove the dough from the refrigerator and cut into 3 to 4 dozen ½-inch-thick slices. (To slice the frozen logs, let thaw for about 5 minutes so they won't crack when you slice them.) Dip each slice into the remaining ¼ cup sugar-*canela* mixture and place on the baking sheets, leaving about 1 inch between slices.

Bake until golden brown, turn over the pastries, and bake for a few more minutes so that both sides are evenly caramelized, 8 to 10 minutes. Let cool on a wire rack.

MAKES 3 TO 4 DOZEN

Garibaldis, orejones, and conchas blancas from Da Silva bakery in Mexico City

Cochinitos de Hojaldre | Puffed Piggies

It's no secret that there is a playfulness in Mexican culture, and it is very apparent in the names and shapes of our sweet breads. One of the most amazing *panaderías* I've ever visited is Horno Los Ortiz in Morelia. The owners are some of the most creative people I've ever met. They spend months shaping dough into intricate figurines that will form a nativity scene like no other. Their signs, specially designed boxes, and skillfully adorned breads for the holidays are remarkable. Their artistry is still present in their daily bread, but on a much simpler and smaller scale. These little pig faces, made from flaky pastry and filled with delicious pastry cream, are similar to ones they were selling during one of my visits. They a very fun project indeed.

Roll out the puff pastry dough on a lightly floured surface to about ¼ inch thick. Cut out ten 6-inch circles and place on parchment-lined baking sheets. Gather the scraps together by placing them on top of each other, overlapping a bit to stick them together (don't form into a ball!). Roll the top lightly to smooth and even it out.

Whip the pastry cream until smooth and divide among 5 of the circles, leaving some room around the edges. Lightly beat the egg yolks with a fork and brush along the edges. Place the remaining 5 circles on top and press tightly along the edges to seal.

Cut out five 2-inch circles for the noses and make two little holes with a toothpick or skewer; attach the noses to the tops of the pastries with some of the egg yolk. To make the ears, cut out 10 circles that are a bit smaller than the nose and pull one side slightly so they are a bit pointy, giving them a bit of movement. Seal with some egg yolk. Refrigerate while you preheat the oven.

Preheat the oven to 375°F.

Mix the remaining egg yolks with the milk and brush the tops of the pastries. Bake until the tops and bottoms are golden, 20 to 30 minutes. Let cool for a few minutes on the baking sheets, then transfer to wire racks to cool completely.

To decorate, spread a little circle of the melted white chocolate to make eyeballs, allow to set, and then put a smaller circle of melted dark chocolate on top of the white to make the center of the eye. Play around and have some fun giving the piggies a personality of their own. (You can put the chocolate in separate plastic syringes or squeeze bottles and put them in the microwave for a few seconds to melt, then squeeze the chocolate onto the pastries.)

SERVES 5

1 recipe Quick Puff Pastry (page 164)

1 recipe Pastry Cream (page 164)

2 egg yolks

1 tablespoon whole milk or heavy cream

2 ounces white chocolate, melted

2 ounces dark chocolate, melted

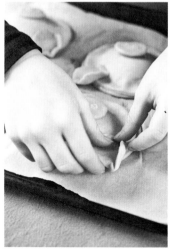

FRUTA

—

FRUIT

FRUITS ARE AN ICONIC SYMBOL of paradise, and in Mexico, we are privileged to have an abundant variety. Their beauty has inspired painters such as Rufino Tamayo and Frida Kahlo, songwriters ("*Naranja dulce, limón partido, dame un abrazo que yo te pido*/Sweet orange, cut lime, give me a hug that I am asking for"), and many poets.

The Latin American poet Bernardo de Balbuena extolled the many uses of Mexican fruits, writing in 1604, "They are placed on the altars of the dead with loving care on the second of November; mixed jicamas, tangerines, sugar cane, *colaciones* (colorful small, rough-shaped sugar balls that are often flavored with aniseseed) and peanuts are hidden in the bellies of piñatas; they are sprinkled with sugar and dried but still shiny in the Rosca de Reyes (Three Kings Bread); or they surprise us underneath the puff pastry in the heart of an empanada . . . " Likewise, Fray Bernardino Sahagún wrote extensively about the markets in Tlatelolco, and Hernán Cortés wrote many detailed letters describing the fruit in the newly discovered lands. Don Artemio de Valle-Arzipe, a Mexican writer and diplomat, depicted a wonderful feast in the early twentieth century (the honoree is unknown) of sweet potato–pineapple *dulce*; *alfeñique* fountains with delicate almond-paste fruits; almond candies covered with cinnamon, morsels of coconut, and pecans; glassy quince; toasted, filled, candied, or "drunk" (in syrup) pears; crystallized peaches; and more.

According to Victor Manuel Toledo, a biologist and researcher, by the time Europeans arrived in Mesoamerica, the inhabitants had domesticated more than sixty varieties of fruit, including avocado, cacao, *capulin*, guava, prickly pear, *zapote blanco*, *amarillo y negro*, *pitahaya* (a beautiful and sensual fruit with a fuchsia skin that encapsulates a white flesh with tiny black seeds), and *tejocote* (a fruit similar to crab apple). Tamarind, cantaloupe, pears, and bananas were brought to Mexico during colonization. And it is believed that coconuts came to Mexico thousands of years before, not by migrants or conquistadors, but rather by floating along on the sea. They found a home in Mexico and were soon abundantly cultivated in all the tropical areas.

The most natural preparation for fruits was in the sweet kitchen, where they were first combined with the sugar the Spaniards brought and later prepared with the French techniques that peaked in the nineteenth century. Although Mexicans ate differently according to their social class, fruit was a part of everyone's daily diet because it was so abundant.

Markets in Mexico are like colorful, fragrant paintings that include ingenious displays of these natural desserts. Fruit sellers know just how to bring out the best in their wares, whether it is the joyful color of incredibly bright and juicy mangoes, the sensuality of papayas, or the soft creaminess of mameys.

Although many fruits can be found all over Mexico, there are regions where only certain fruits grow. The enormous diversity of fruit can be overwhelming, but I want to mention a few of the most interesting ones.

The *biznaga*, for example, refers to two types of cactus, and the edible part, known as *cabuches*, looks a bit like asparagus tips. It is mainly used to prepare *acitrón*. (Originally the *biznaga* was cooked to concentrate the natural sugars in the plant, then mixed with *aguamiel* and sold as candy in the markets of Tlatelolco. After colonization, *acitrón* was prepared with sugarcane instead, and made primarily by the nuns.) *Cabuches* are cooked in syrup and have a wonderful natural sweetness; they are sold in cups in markets in central Mexico. *Acitrón*, sold in cubes or rectangles, can be found all over Mexico and is used in meat fillings, sweet tamales, and Rosca de Reyes, or eaten by itself.

Capulines, which are native to Mexico, were mistaken for a kind of cherry by the Spaniards because they are small, round, and dark purple (almost black), but with no stem. Abundant throughout the summer, they

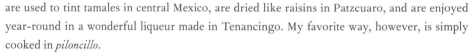

are used to tint tamales in central Mexico, are dried like raisins in Patzcuaro, and are enjoyed year-round in a wonderful liqueur made in Tenancingo. My favorite way, however, is simply cooked in *piloncillo*.

Marañón is the fruit from the cashew nut plant. The meaty flesh is a bit tart and lightly sweet. The fruit grows wild in southeast Mexico and can be blended with some water and sugar for an *agua fresca* or made into preserves, particularly in Campeche and Quintana Roo. There are many other regional fruits that are sold as preserves, and it's a good way to try a whole new palette of flavors.

Many parts of the fruit are used in Mexican sweets. The skin serves as a base for liqueurs, and the hearts are used to ferment beverages or are dried and used medicinally. The leaves are used to wrap tamales or other treats and to flavor or enhance a sauce. The flesh is often puréed for a sweet preparation, and whole fruits are left to adorn the table and stimulate the appetite.

Fruits abound everywhere in Mexico, and as you walk through the markets, their sweet, ripe juices fill the air. They are part of our daily lives and celebrations. Their essence is encased in a brilliant shield of crystallized sugar; they mingle with other rich ingredients in ice creams; their forms are lovingly sculpted from sweet marzipan paste; they are captured through time in a bottle; and they are simply bitten, torn, scooped, or cut. No matter how they are prepared, they are nutritious, natural, and incredibly delicious sweets.

2 pounds fresh fruit such as pineapple, prickly pear, papaya, chayote, plums, or figs

2 quarts water

¼ cup calcium oxide

5½ cups sugar

Crystallized fruit is basically fruit that's been cooked for a long time in a sugar or *piloncillo* syrup until it is almost translucent (hence the name). It is customary to presoak the fruit overnight in lime or calcium oxide so that it retains its shape after the long cooking process. The town of Santa Cruz Acalpixa in Xochimilco is one of the best places to appreciate the enormous variety of candied fruit, including prickly pears, figs, oranges, cactus paddles, and even chiles. A word of caution, though: beware of bees when making this!

The process takes several days, but it's quite simple and the fruit will last for a several months and up to a year if stored properly. You can use the same method for many kinds of fruit, so pick some that are in season but slightly underripe so they don't fall apart.

Wash the fruit, peel, and slice if necessary (leave small fruits such as figs, plums, and prickly pears whole). Prick the fruit in a few places with a skewer or needle (sterilize the needle by heating it over a flame for a couple of minutes).

Combine the water and calcium oxide in a large bowl and stir to dissolve. Add the fruit. Allow to soak overnight in a dry place. Strain and rinse the fruit very well under cold water.

Place the fruit in a large pot and add cold water to cover. Add 4½ cups of the sugar and cook at a constant soft simmer, without letting it come to a boil, for 1 hour. Remove from the heat, cover the pot with a lid, and allow to sit overnight.

Add ½ cup of the remaining sugar to the pot and bring to a boil. Reduce the heat to maintain a simmer and cook for 1 hour. Remove from the heat, cover the pot with a lid, and allow to sit overnight. Repeat the same process the next day with the remaining ½ cup sugar.

Remove the fruit with a slotted spoon and drain on a wire rack. Cook the remaining syrup over medium heat until it has reduced to a thick, honeylike consistency, about 5 minutes. Pour the syrup over the fruit while still on the rack. Allow to dry out in the sun for 1 to 2 days. Store in an airtight container in a cool, dry place for up to 1 year.

MAKES 2 POUNDS

Cocada | Coconut Caramel Candy

There are countless sweets made from shredded or ground coconut, called *cocadas*. Some are cooked with milk and baked; others are mixed with *piloncillo*, thickened with eggs, and finished with liqueur or simply cooked in their own juice. How to choose one recipe? This was no easy task, but I chose this particular one from a small village in Yucatan, where I found a stand that sold more than twenty different kinds. The fresh lime zest brightens the slightly burnt flavor of the caramel that enrobes the tasty coconut morsels. This could even be used as a sort of jam if cooked a little less. For a little more information on coconut, see page 9.

1½ cups sugar

⅓ cup water

1¼ cups coconut water

2 cups fresh shaved coconut

Pinch of salt

Zest of 1 lime

Combine the sugar and water in a small heavy pot. Place the pot over medium heat and cover; when you hear the mixture boiling, remove the lid (the steam helps to prevent the sugar from crystallizing). Continue cooking without stirring, until it begins to turn golden. At this point, you can swirl the caramel around so that it caramelizes evenly, and then continue cooking until it is a dark caramel color.

Remove from the heat and add the coconut water, whisking or stirring carefully because it will sizzle and steam, and then return to the heat. Once the caramel is smooth again, add the shaved coconut and salt and bring to a boil over medium heat. Reduce the heat to maintain a simmer and cook, stirring, until it starts to thicken and you can see the bottom of the pot when scraped with a spoon, about 40 minutes. Remove from the heat and add the lime zest.

Let sit until cool enough to handle, moisten your hand with a little bit of water, then shape into little pyramids. These will be a bit sticky, so put a piece of parchment paper underneath them. Store in an airtight container in a cool, dry area for up to 1 month.

MAKES ABOUT 1 DOZEN

Pelliscos de Tamarindo Acapulqueño | Tamarind Candy Balls

As my friend Josefina says, we Mexicans love two kinds of sweets: the really over-the-top sweet, sticky ones that make your teeth ache, and the tart-spicy ones that make your mouth pucker, scorch your palate, and make the tip of your tongue salivate. Many of these latter kinds are made with tamarind.

This recipe is one that most people think of when it comes to *dulce de tamarindo*. They are sold along the highways and beaches of Acapulco. Even when they are mixed with sugar, they remain tart and acidic; however, I have included an option for adding citric acid for those who really want an extreme puckery sensation.

These tamarind balls have seeds in them. You can make them without the seeds, but it's a little extra work (however, I don't think you'll mind sucking the seeds, trying to get all the tasty candy off).

Remove the outer hard shell from the tamarind pods and remove the strings that are attached to it. Put the cleaned tamarinds and the water in a medium saucepan. Combine the sugar and citric acid in a small bowl, then add to the saucepan. Cook over medium heat, stirring, until the sugar is dissolved, the mixture is thick, and you can see the bottom of the pot when scraped with a spoon, 20 to 25 minutes. Remove from the heat and let sit until cool enough to handle.

FOR THE SPICY TAMARINDS, combine the sugar, chile powders, and salt and knead into the tamarind mixture as if you were making bread. Roll into golf ball–size balls, then wrap each ball in clear cellophane and store in an airtight container.

FOR THE SWEET TAMARINDS, combine ¾ cup of the sugar with the salt and knead into the tamarind mixture as if you were making bread. Roll into golf ball–size balls, roll in the remaining ¼ cup sugar, then wrap each ball in clear cellophane and store in an airtight container.

MAKES 1 DOZEN

NOTE: For the pelliscos, you can use 12 ounces tamarind purée in place of the whole fresh tamarinds, but make sure it has no added sugar or anything else. You may find it in Latin or ethnic food markets; it is sometimes called "wet tamarind." Check the date to make sure it's fresh, and make sure the seeds inside are not black (sometimes they are burned during manufacture). You can cook them the same way you would fresh tamarind.

1 pound tamarind pods (the ones from Latin America tend to have a more tart flavor than the ones from Thailand; see Note)

¾ cup water

1 cup sugar

1 teaspoon citric acid (optional)

Spicy Finish

⅓ cup sugar

1 teaspoon ground guajillo chile

½ teaspoon ground piquín or cayenne chile

¼ teaspoon salt

Sweet Finish

1 cup sugar

¼ teaspoon salt

VARIATION: CANDIED TAMARIND

Another idea is to peel the tamarinds, leaving them whole, then add to a saucepan with 1 cup water and 1 cup sugar. Place over medium heat to dissolve the sugar, and simmer until they are just soft, about 12 minutes. Let dry on a wire rack, then roll in sugar and allow to set. It's quick and lovely.

Corteza de Toronja Confitada | Candied Grapefruit Peels

This is a four-generation recipe that is still enjoyed today by Estela Elizondo's family in Monterrey, Mexico. I have made these many times and really like them. If you like a little heat, toss them with about 1 teaspoon ground chile, such as chipotle or guajillo, mixed with the superfine sugar. To me, that makes these traditional strips of sweetness have a little fun while dancing along on your palate. You can use the leftover grapefruit flesh to make the Red Sorbet Terrine with Hibiscus Compote (page 196).

4 thick-skinned grapefruits

3 cups granulated sugar

1¾ cups water

½ cup superfine sugar

Slice the ends off the grapefruits and make a lengthwise slit with the knife. Peel the skin from the flesh with your hands. Reserve the flesh for another use. Cut the skin with scissors or a knife into strips about ⅓ inch wide.

Place the strips in a pot and cover with about 2 quarts cold water, bring to a boil over high heat, strain, and repeat 4 more times.

Combine the granulated sugar with the 1¾ cups water in a pot and cook over medium-high heat until the sugar has dissolved, about 5 minutes. Add the strained grapefruit strips and stir lightly. Simmer for 10 minutes, then let cool for 10 minutes. Drain in a sieve until almost dry but still sticky, about 4 hours. Toss in the superfine sugar.

Store in an airtight container in a dry, cool place for up to 1 month.

MAKES ABOUT 4 CUPS

Duraznos en Almibar | Peaches in Syrup

These sweet peaches are used often in Mexican cooking primarily to decorate cakes and to eat with ice cream or pancakes. I thought it might be nice to have this recipe so you can make some at the height of peach season and use them in the colder months when fresh local ones are out of the question.

½ pound yellow peaches

½ cup sugar

Prepare an ice bath. Bring a large pot of water to a boil. Carefully place the peaches in the boiling water for 10 seconds, then remove with a slotted spoon and place them in the ice bath. Pour out the boiling water, reserving 1 cup. Add the sugar to the water and cook, stirring, until the sugar dissolves.

Meanwhile, carefully peel the peaches and cut in half lengthwise, discarding the pits. Put the peaches in a sterilized jar, leaving at least

½ inch at the top. Pour the syrup over the peaches and run a knife or spatula around the edges to remove excess bubbles. Tightly cover and refrigerate for up to 2 months.

If you want to keep the peaches longer, up to a year, you will need to can them. Make sure you use a mason jar, then put the sealed jars in a canner, fill with about 2 inches of water, and cook for 30 to 45 minutes, depending on the altitude (the higher it is, the longer you'll need). Lift the jars carefully and let cool completely in a dry area. Once the jars have cooled, make sure that the tops are well sealed by pressing the centers lightly. They shouldn't pop.

MAKES ABOUT 1 QUART

Tejocotes en Almibar | Tejocotes in Syrup

1 pound fresh or frozen *tejocotes* (see Sources)

2 cups sugar

1 (3-inch) stick *canela*

2 allspice berries

Tejocotes are small fruits similar to crab apples but are quite sour and have inedible seeds. The name derives from the word *texocotl*, meaning "sour, wild, or hard fruit," and they are abundant at the end of the year. My maternal grandmother, Juanita, used to make this delicious treat and always reserved a huge jar just for me.

Rinse the *tejocotes* under cold water, add to a saucepan, and add water to cover. Bring to a boil over high heat, then adjust the heat so the mixture is just barely simmering. Cook until tender and the skins begin to puff or separate, 15 to 20 minutes. Drain, reserving the liquid, and let sit until cool enough to handle. Peel the *tejocotes* and remove the seeds very carefully with the tip of a knife.

Return the fruits to the pot with the cooking liquid, and add the sugar, *canela*, and allspice. Cook over medium heat, maintaining a soft boil, until fully cooked and the syrup has thickened, 45 to 60 minutes. Remove from the heat and let cool completely. Divide the *tejocotes* among serving bowls and drizzle some of the syrup over each.

MAKES ABOUT 1¹/₂ QUARTS

Guayabate | Guava Caramel Pecan Rolls

Guava is one of the most sensual fruits, and it truly shines when it's cooked. Filled with luscious caramel and toasted pecans, this treat defines sinful. Look for guavas that are soft to the touch and fragrant. You can also find them frozen or puréed, but make sure they're not loaded with sugar or anything else.

Cover the guavas with water in a medium nonreactive pot and cook over medium heat until soft, 10 to 15 minutes. Let cool slightly, and then purée the guava in a food processor. Strain to remove the seeds and measure 2 cups.

Combine the guava purée and the sugar in the nonreactive pot over medium heat, adjusting the heat to maintain a constant simmer, stirring constantly, until the mixture is thick and you can see the bottom of the pot when scraped with a spoon, about 30 minutes. Add the lemon juice and stir to combine.

Turn a baking sheet upside down, spray lightly with oil, place a piece of parchment paper on top, and dust lightly with sugar. Pour the cooked guava mixture onto the baking sheet and spread with an offset spatula to about ½ inch thick. Allow to cool to the touch until it doesn't feel sticky, 40 to 50 minutes, then spread on the *cajeta* to about ½ inch from the edges. Sprinkle the pecans all over. Roll tightly away from you until you reach the center, then cut along the rolled edge. Repeat with the remaining half so you have 2 rolls. Allow to set, and cut into slices as desired. To store, wrap in parchment paper and then in plastic wrap. Store in a dry, cool area for up to 1 month.

MAKES 2

NOTE: If you can't find fresh guavas (or just want to save a bit of time), look for prepared guava paste called *ate*, which is available at Latin and specialty markets. Cut the paste into pieces and place in a double boilder over medium heat. Allow the paste to "melt," stirring frequently and pressing it against the sides until smooth.

1⅓ pounds guavas, cleaned

2 cups sugar, plus more for dusting

1 tablespoon freshly squeezed lemon juice

¾ cup *cajeta*, homemade (page 151) or store-bought

½ cup coarsely chopped toasted pecans

VARIATION: GUAVA ROLL-UPS

Let the guava mixture cool on the baking sheet, without adding the *cajeta* and nuts, then slice into long strips and roll up.

VARIATION: GUAVA PASTE

Pour the guava mixture into a lightly oiled mold or ceramic serving dish, cover, and allow to set at room temperature.

VARIATION: MANGO CARAMEL PECAN ROLLS

To use mangoes instead of guavas, peel the mangoes, cook in boiling water for 5 minutes, then let cool. Remove the flesh and purée, strain, and then measure out 2 cups and proceed with the recipe.

Rollo de Datil y Nuez | Date-Pecan Roll

My mother's friend Yoya Estrada is one of the sweetest ladies I've ever met, and she transmits her kindness through her hands. She shared this family recipe from Durango with me a few years ago, and it's one of my favorites. It lasts awhile if it's well wrapped. Enjoy it sliced on its own or serve it with an assortment of cheeses, even though that is not the traditional Mexican way.

3 cups pitted dates
(about 1 pound)

4 cups pecans (about 1 pound)

1½ cups sugar, plus extra
for rolling

½ cup water

Coarsely chop the dates with a lightly oiled knife. Place in a heavy pot and add the pecans, sugar, and water and cook over low-medium heat, stirring, until the dates have fallen apart and you can see the bottom of the pot when scraped with a spoon, 10 to 15 minutes. The mixture will be thick and you will feel it in your arm! Remove from the heat and allow to cool slightly.

Meanwhile, dampen 2 large pieces (about 14 by 18 inches) of cheesecloth, and squeeze out the excess water. Lay out one of the cheesecloths and spread one-fourth of the mixture along the bottom (centered). Roll tightly into a log and remove the cheesecloth. Repeat with the remaining mixture to roll 3 more logs. (Use the second cheesecloth if the first one becomes too sticky or breaks.) Roll the logs in sugar and wrap well in plastic wrap, then put inside a resealable bag. Keep in a cool, dry area. The rolls can last up to 3 months stored this way. They may seem hard at first but once you slice them, you'll see they are still delicious.

MAKES 4 (10-OUNCE) LOGS

Jam Filling

4 cups cherry tomatoes

1¼ cups sugar

Pinch of salt

Empanada Dough

2 cups all-purpose flour

½ teaspoon baking powder

3 tablespoons sugar

Pinch of salt

¾ cup unsalted butter, cut into small cubes

½ cup *crema* or heavy cream, plus extra for topping

Egg yolk, for topping

Sugar, for topping

When I visited the city of Monterrey, a family friend, Amado, lovingly and kindly drove me around, showing me the wonderful delicacies of the surrounding towns. He took me to the small town of Marin where Martha Chapa has a small shop famous for her cookies, where I tried an amazing tomato empanada that I couldn't stop thinking about. She told me how to make the jam, and, when she saw how excited I was, she gave me a large container filled with it. I kept eating spoonfuls of it on my way home and adapted the recipe once I was back in my kitchen. You can keep the jam chunky, or, if you like a smoother consistency, you can pulse it in a food processor after it's cooked. The jam can be made well in advance and will keep for months if properly stored. It is very tasty on its own and I recommend that you make a big batch.

TO MAKE THE FILLING, wash and dry the tomatoes. Cut the tomatoes in half and place them in a small, heavy pot with the sugar and salt. Bring the mixture to a boil and adjust the heat so that it is at a constant simmer. Cook, stirring often, until the jam is thickened and you can see the bottom of the pot, about 50 minutes. (If you want a very smooth jam, you can pulse it in a food processor.) Let cool before using.

TO MAKE THE DOUGH, whisk together the flour, baking powder, sugar, and salt in a medium bowl. Using a pastry cutter or a food processor, cut the butter into the dry mixture until it resembles a coarse meal. Add the cream and mix until just combined. Invert the dough onto a lightly floured work surface and knead until it is smooth and uniform, about 2 to 3 minutes. Flatten to a disc, wrap in plastic wrap, and refrigerate for at least half an hour.

Roll out the dough on a lightly floured surface, with a lightly floured rolling pin, until ⅛ inch thick. Use a round cookie cutter to cut out 4- to 5-inch diameter circles; gather the scraps, re-roll, and repeat until all of the dough is used up.

To form the empanadas, line up the dough circles on a lightly floured work surface. Place about 1 tablespoon of the filling in the center of each dough circle. Fold half of the dough over the filling, then press the edges very lightly with your fingers to seal; you can fold the sealed edge toward the center to give it a decorative finish. Alternatively, use the back of a fork to press around the edge to seal the empanada. Cut 2 small slits in the top of each turnover and refrigerate for 30 minutes.

CONTINUED

Meanwhile, preheat the oven to 350°F. Whisk one yolk with a little cream and top with sugar. Bake until they are golden brown and cool in rack. These may be eaten warm or cold.

MAKES 12 TO 16

NOTE: For a delicious, quick filling, cut a few cubes of guava paste (page 131 or store-bought) and mix with a little *queso fresco* or *requesón* to fill these flaky empanadas.

2 teaspoons baking soda

12 medium-large limes, rinsed well

2½ cups sugar

Green food coloring (optional)

2 cups shredded fresh coconut

½ cup water

The coast of Colima, a small state in southwest Mexico, is renowned for many candies, particularly coconut ones. The vibrant candied limes retain a slight bitterness that contrasts nicely with the sweet coconut filling. Eating them will make you feel like you are walking along the beach.

Bring 2 quarts of water to a boil over high heat, add 1 teaspoon of the baking soda, stir to combine, and then add the limes. Cook at a soft simmer until slightly tender, 10 to 15 minutes. Remove the limes from the water with a slotted spoon and let cool.

Make a small incision in the top of each lime with a sharp paring knife and carefully scrape out the flesh, making sure you don't tear the rind; discard the filling. Return the intact rinds to the pot, add cold water to cover, and stir in the remaining 1 teaspoon baking soda. Bring to a boil, strain, and repeat this process (without any more baking soda) 3 more times to remove the bitterness from the limes.

Return the limes to the pot, add cold water to cover, then stir in 1½ cups of the sugar and a few drops of food coloring. Cook over medium-low heat, stirring, until the syrup has thickened to the consistency of corn or maple syrup, 15 to 20 minutes. Remove from the heat, let cool completely in the syrup, then transfer the limes to a wire rack and let dry.

Combine the coconut, the remaining 1 cup sugar, and the ½ cup water in a saucepan and cook over medium heat, stirring, until the coconut is soft, almost translucent, and thick. Let cool until it is safe to handle.

Fill the limes with the coconut mixture and let cool completely. Eat by biting into the lime. Store in an airtight container lined with parchment paper in a cool, dry place for up to 2 months.

MAKES 12

Gelatina de Naranja con Leche | Orange and Milk Gelatin

Brightly colored gelatins filled with different layers—translucent or pastel—and over-the-top gelatin figurines are sold everywhere in Mexico. I couldn't have a book on Mexican sweets without at least one gelatin, so I picked one that has familiar flavors. Think of it like a Creamsicle in a whole new presentation.

This recipe is based on one from a book by Josefina Velázquez de León. Make sure you use fresh oranges for the best flavor.

TO MAKE THE VANILLA GELATIN, combine the egg yolks, sugar, and milk in a medium heavy pot. Scrape the vanilla bean into the pot, add the pod, and cook over medium heat, stirring, until it starts to boil. Remove from the heat and allow to cool for 10 minutes. Remove and discard the pod. (If the mixture curdles and looks a bit like scrambled eggs, simply blend with a handheld mixer or pour into a blender.)

Sprinkle the gelatin over the water in a small bowl and let sit for a couple of minutes to soften. Add to the warm custard, stirring until the gelatin dissolves. Pour into 8 glasses, filling almost halfway up. Refrigerate until set, 2 to 3 hours.

TO MAKE THE ORANGE GELATIN, combine ¾ cup of the orange juice and the sugar in a medium saucepan over low heat, and cook, stirring, until the sugar dissolves, 5 to 7 minutes. Remove from the heat.

Sprinkle the gelatin over the water in a small bowl and let sit for a couple of minutes to soften. Add to the warm juice and sugar mixture, stirring until the gelatin dissolves. Add the remaining 1 cup orange juice and stir to combine. Pour over the vanilla gelatin (once it's completely set) and refrigerate until fully set, 2 to 3 hours.

SERVES 8

Vanilla Gelatin

2 egg yolks

¾ cup sugar

2 cups whole milk

1 vanilla bean, split lengthwise

1 tablespoon powdered gelatin

¼ cup cold water

Orange Gelatin

1¾ cups freshly squeezed orange juice

⅔ cup sugar

1 tablespoon powdered gelatin

¼ cup water

VARIATION: ROMPOPE GELATIN

You can use Rompope (page 32) in place of the vanilla gelatin for added depth of flavor. Make the rompope as directed, then follow the recipe above from step 2 on.

Dulce de Zapote Negro | Black Zapote Pudding

½ pound black *zapote* fruits

¾ cup freshly squeezed orange juice

1 tablespoon freshly squeezed lime juice

½ cup sugar

¼ cup rum (optional)

Orange segments, for garnish

Whipped cream, for garnish

The black *zapote* fruit got its name because the inside pulp is actually black like mud, but don't be put off by the unusual color because the fruit is succulent and sweet. If you are in a place where you can get them, buy the ones that feel so soft as to seem almost spoiled, because these have the best flavor. The creamy pulp blends very nicely with the fresh orange juice and is a classic combination.

Cut the *zapotes* in half and scoop out the pulp (discard the skin and any seeds). Combine with the orange juice, lime juice, sugar, and rum in a blender or mix by hand in a bowl until very smooth. Pour into 8 glasses or serving dishes and refrigerate, covered, for at least 3 hours so the flavors blend together. Garnish with a few orange segments and a dollop of whipped cream and serve.

SERVES 8

Dulce de Mamey | Mamey Fruit Cream

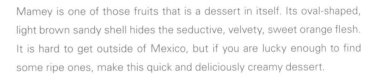

2 mamey fruits

1½ cups heavy cream

½ teaspoon pure vanilla extract

6 tablespoons superfine sugar

Mamey is one of those fruits that is a dessert in itself. Its oval-shaped, light brown sandy shell hides the seductive, velvety, sweet orange flesh. It is hard to get outside of Mexico, but if you are lucky enough to find some ripe ones, make this quick and deliciously creamy dessert.

Cut each mamey in half lengthwise and set aside one-fourth of one of the mamey fruits for garnish. Discard the seed, then scoop out the pulp and purée in a blender or food processor. Pour into a bowl. Whip the heavy cream with the vanilla until beginning to thicken, 3 to 5 minutes, then add the sugar and continue to mix until it has thickened and soft peaks form (lift a bit of the whipped cream and when the peaks fall a bit, it's ready), about 5 minutes. Fold 1 cup of the whipped cream (refrigerate the rest for later) into the mamey purée until fully incorporated, and then pour it into individual glasses or dessert dishes. Refrigerate for at least 1 hour to set. Slice the reserved mamey. Garnish with the remaining ½ cup whipped cream (re-whip if necessary) and the mamey slices.

SERVES 6

POSTRES

DESSERTS

DESSERTS IN GENERAL could be defined as a sweet course served at the end of a meal. In Mexico, this is a tradition we inherited from Europe.

Lunch in Mexico is the biggest meal of the day, followed by the wonderful *sobremesa*, the endless lingering that goes on after a meal, a tradition that is said to have begun in the 1930s. Coffee, tea, or liqueur is often served and accompanied by a few cookies, a tray of confections, crystallized fruit, or assorted candies. Desserts such as layered cakes, pies, and tortes are not that common and are left for a special occasion or eaten when you go out.

Although, the distinction between candies, confections, and desserts is hard to describe, this section includes desserts that are found in most typical restaurants and are familiar to many, as well as other specialties that could be served at the end of any Mexican feast (though, in my humble opinion, most sweets in this book can be served that way).

Many Latin American countries claim that the origin of rice pudding or flan is theirs, but the truth is that they were brought by the Spaniards and many of their recipes are of Arab origin. Why, then, would they be included in a book on Mexican sweets? Because, as with many other things, we adopted them into our culture, and they are prepared and enjoyed all over Mexico. The distinction or definition of authenticity is one that is intimately linked with *mestizaje*—the melding or blending of the two cultures.

Dairy products and sugar (from cane) did not exist before the Spaniards arrived, and many of these desserts—and the book as a whole, for that matter—would not exist without these two staples. After Independence, Mexicans searched for identity, and many quickly embraced the new influence of France. French ingredients and baking techniques are therefore very apparent in many of the desserts in this chapter. Although relations between France and Mexico did not end well, the love for French pastries has continued unabated. Their flaky pastries, silky creams, delicate elegance, and beautiful presentation captured Mexicans the moment they arrived.

Likewise, this chapter will grab you with its creamy custards, cinnamon-scented rice pudding, wonderfully moist tres leches cake, and *crepas de cajeta*, my absolute favorite dessert.

Pastel de Tres Leches | Tres Leches Cake   •

There are many versions of this popular cake, but I find most to be too heavy, overly sweet, and not moist enough. After much experimenting, I found the one that I think produces an incredibly moist, lighter version. This chiffonlike cake soaks up a lot of milk, which gives it a kind of "melt in your mouth" quality, without being mushy. The rum adds even more moistness, helps cut the sweetness, and provides another layer of flavor. Because of the amount of liquid, the cake might seep a little, so be sure to refrigerate it until you serve it.

This is also a recipe that you can make your own. You can substitute coconut milk for the condensed milk, adding some coconut liqueur instead of rum; use different fruits in the filling; or omit the rum in the soaking liquid and add it to the whipped cream at the end, for example. You could also soak it with *rompope* instead of the triple milk mixture, or make a four-milk cake and finish it with *cajeta* or *dulce de leche*.

To make an over-the-top cake, the kind that is tall and bold and makes a statement, double the recipe and bake the cake in two 9-inch pans. Slice the tops and follow the same procedure, but soak the cakes for a bit longer. Either way, this cake is a celebratory dessert and a sure crowd-pleaser.

Preheat the oven to 350°F. Grease an 8-inch cake pan. Put a circle of parchment paper on the bottom of the pan, grease lightly, and flour the bottom and sides, tapping out the excess flour.

TO MAKE THE CAKE, place the flour, 6 tablespoons of the sugar, the baking powder, and the salt in a large bowl and whisk to combine. In a separate bowl, mix the egg yolks with the vegetable oil, water, and vanilla until thoroughly combined.

In a clean, dry bowl, beat the egg whites with the cream of tartar until they start to thicken but have not reached soft peaks. Gradually add the remaining 6 tablespoons sugar and continue to beat until stiff, but not dry, peaks form.

Add one-fourth of the flour mixture to the egg-yolk mixture and blend well. Add one-fourth of the beaten egg whites and fold gently. Repeat, alternating the flour mixture and the beaten egg whites, finishing with the egg whites, until thoroughly combined.

Pour into the prepared pan and bake until the top springs back when touched and a toothpick inserted into the center comes out clean, 35 to 45 minutes.

Cake

1 cup all-purpose flour

¾ cup granulated sugar

1½ teaspoons baking powder

Pinch of salt

4 eggs, separated, at room temperature

¼ cup vegetable oil

2 tablespoons water

¼ teaspoon pure vanilla extract

½ teaspoon cream of tartar

Tres Leches

1 cup heavy cream

1 (12-ounce) can evaporated milk

1 teaspoon pure vanilla extract

Pinch of salt

1 (14-ounce) can sweetened condensed milk

½ cup dark rum (optional but highly recommended)

Filling

1⅓ cups heavy cream

¼ cup confectioner's sugar

½ teaspoon pure vanilla extract, or ½ vanilla bean, scraped

1 to 2 cups coarsely chopped or sliced fresh fruit (strawberries, mangoes, and/or canned peaches are commonly used)

CONTINUED

Allow to cool slightly, then turn out onto a wire rack. Remove the parchment paper and let cool completely. Gently slice the top to even it out and slice in half widthwise with a serrated knife.

TO MAKE THE TRES LECHES, combine the heavy cream, evaporated milk, vanilla, and salt in a medium pot and scald over medium heat. Remove from the heat and whisk in the condensed milk and rum, blending well. Put the cakes in a deep dish and pour the warm mixture over them. Be sure to pour any liquid that dripped down the sides on top of the cake as well. Cover with plastic wrap and refrigerate for 1 hour, or freeze for 30 to 40 minutes, so they are easier to handle.

TO MAKE THE FILLING, beat the heavy cream with an electric mixer or by hand until slightly thickened. Add the confectioner's sugar and vanilla and continue beating until thickened and smooth. Refrigerate until the cakes have cooled.

To assemble the cake, put one of the cakes on a piece of cardboard or a serving platter and spread one-third of the whipped cream evenly on top. Cover with most of the chopped fruit, reserving some for decorating. Top with the second cake and cover the top and sides with the remaining whipped cream. Decorate with the reserved fruit as desired. Dip a knife into hot water before cutting each slice.

SERVES 8 TO 10

ITALIAN MERINGUE

Try this luscious topping on the cake above instead of the whipped cream. Finish by toasting the meringue waves with a kitchen torch.

Combine the sugar and water in a small pan and cover and cook over low-medium heat. Once you can hear it boiling, remove the lid (the steam will help avoid crystallization). Continue cooking, without stirring until you reach the soft-ball stage (see page 13).

Meanwhile, in a large heatproof bowl, whip together the egg whites, cream of tartar, and salt to medium peaks. Add the syrup in a stream and continue to whip until the bowl feels cool to the touch.

Meringue for Filling

If I'm using the Italian Meringue as a filling for *gaznates* or other treats, I like to dress it up a little more.

Red food coloring (optional)
3 tablespoons mezcal

Prepare the meringue as directed below, but add the red food coloring to the hot syrup once the sugar has dissolved (the meringue should be bright pink) and stir in the mezcal once all the syrup has been added. Finish by toasting the meringue waves with a kitchen torch. Dip a knife into hot water before making each slice so the meringue doesn't stick to it.

1 cup sugar

⅓ cup water

5 egg whites, at room temperature

½ teaspoon cream of tartar

Pinch of salt

4 cups whole milk

1 (3-inch) piece *canela*

⅓ cup sugar

5 egg yolks

½ teaspoon pure vanilla extract

Pinch of salt

When I visited Guadalajara, I spent two whole days asking around and traveling to find the best *jericallas* possible. I came across a lot of misguided information and dead ends, but eventually, persistence and curiosity paid off. I found a little shop with an eggshell-colored metal wall and a tiny opening that allowed you to peek at the rectangular black oven and endless trays of individual glasses, small and large, filled with the yellowish custard. The owner didn't share the recipe; however, she did say that although cornstarch is often used to stabilize it (and she admitted to using it when the price of eggs goes up), the best ones are made without it.

Jericalla is one of my favorite desserts. It's most commonly found in the state of Jalisco, and some say the name derives from the Valencian city of Jérica, where the recipe was brought by Spanish settlers in the eighteenth century. It is similar to flan but lighter (it can't be unmolded), is flavored with *canela*, has a dark toasty sheet on top, and is eaten directly from the cooking vessel. This recipe does not refrigerate well because the topping becomes very unappealing, so it should be eaten the day you make it and at room temperature or briefly chilled.

Preheat the oven to 325°F. Butter 8 ramekins.

Combine the milk, *canela*, and sugar in a pot, bring to a boil over medium heat, and remove from the heat. Let cool for 10 minutes. Remove and discard the *canela*.

In a separate bowl, whisk the egg yolks and then add about 1 cup of the warm milk, whisking continuously. Return to the pot and add the vanilla and salt.

Place the ramekins in a towel-lined baking dish to prevent them from sliding, and fill them with the custard. Fill the baking dish about three-fourths of the way up the sides of the baking dish with hot water. Bake, uncovered, until the tops start to bubble and are dark brown, 25 to 30 minutes. Remove from the oven, remove the ramekins from the baking dish, and let cool to room temperature or chill briefly before serving.

SERVES 8

Flan a la Antigua | Old-Fashioned Flan

During my research, I visited some friends in Chihuahua. We made a family recipe for flan that required raw milk, took ten hours to bake, and sat in the fridge for two days before unmolding! It was, I have to say, the best flan I've ever tasted, but for practicality, I chose a recipe that doesn't require three days of preparation—not to mention living or traveling to a state where raw milk is legal.

The types of flans that exist are endless, and choosing one basic one was no easy task. I could write a whole book on flans (hey, there's an idea!), but, inspired by the gentle patience required by the one in Chihuahua, I chose to do an old-fashioned one. Old-fashioned in the sense that I didn't want to use any canned milk, powders, or artificial flavorings. I also wanted to make a flan that was not too *eggy* because that is a common complaint with these kinds of flans, so I used half-and-half instead of milk to help thicken it.

1¾ cups sugar

¼ cup water

2 cups half-and-half

1 large piece *canela*, or ½ vanilla bean (depending on personal preference)

5 large egg yolks

1 teaspoon pure vanilla extract

Pinch of salt

Preheat the oven to 350°F.

Combine 1 cup of the sugar and the water in a small, heavy saucepan and cook over low-medium heat until the sugar dissolves and turns a dark golden color (once it starts changing color, swirl it around so it caramelizes evenly). Divide among 6 ramekins and swirl around to coat the bottoms.

Combine the half-and-half and *canela* (if using vanilla, split lengthwise with the tip of a knife and add the seeds and the pod) in a saucepan and bring to a simmer over medium heat. Remove from the heat and cover. Allow to steep for 15 minutes to extract the flavor. Meanwhile, mix together the egg yolks, the remaining ¾ cup sugar, the vanilla, and the salt in a large heatproof mixing bowl placed on a towel to keep it from wobbling while whisking in the hot liquid. Slowly ladle about 1 cup of the hot infused milk into the egg mixture while whisking. Add the egg mixture back to the milk while you whisk gently (try to prevent excess air bubbles from forming). Strain and use right away or chill it over an ice bath to use another day (it can be made up to 3 days ahead).

Place the prepared ramekins evenly spaced in a towel-lined baking dish to keep them from sliding. Divide the mixture among the ramekins and pop any bubbles with a spoon. Carefully pour hot water to fill three-fourths of the way up sides of the baking dish and cover loosely with aluminum foil (you can also make a few holes in the foil to prevent steaming). Bake until the flans are set around the edges but slightly jiggly in the center, about 30 minutes. Remove the baking dish from the oven and remove the ramekins with a towel or tongs. Let cool, uncovered, until they feel cool to the touch and then chill in the refrigerator for at least 6 hours (this can be done a day in advance).

To unmold, fill a bowl or small pot with 2 to 3 inches of very hot water. Dip a small, sharp knife in the hot water, dry it quickly, and run it around the edges of the ramekins. Dip the bottoms of the ramekins into the hot water for about 20 seconds and unmold onto a plate. The flan should slowly unmold but if it feels a bit stuck, run a knife around the edges once again. Serve chilled or at room temperature.

SERVES 6

Arroz con Leche | Rice Pudding

1 cup short- or medium-grain rice

2 cups water

3 cups whole milk

1 cup heavy cream

1 large piece *canela*

½ vanilla bean, scraped, or 2 long strips lime or lemon zest

¼ teaspoon salt

⅓ cup sugar

¾ cup dark raisins (optional)

Freshly ground, toasted *canela*, for sprinkling

This is probably one of the most well-known Mexican desserts, even though it is believed to have Middle Eastern/Persian origins and is found throughout the world in many variations, such as coconut, almond, and orange. The heavy cream gives it a rich mouthfeel and reminds me of the raw milk found in Mexico. This dish is adapted from an old recipe I found in a cookbook without any date or author.

Combine the rice and water in a pot and bring to a boil over medium heat. Cook for a few minutes, stirring occasionally, until the water is almost gone and you can see the bottom of the pot when scraped with a spoon, about 5 minutes. Add the milk, cream, *canela*, vanilla bean with the pod, and the salt. Bring to a boil over medium heat, stirring occasionally so it doesn't stick to the bottom. Add the sugar, adjust the heat to maintain a constant soft simmer, and cook until the rice is soft, 20 to 30 minutes. Add the raisins and cook for about 5 minutes longer. Remove from the heat, discard the vanilla pod and the *canela*, and allow to cool. (You can place a layer of plastic wrap directly on top to prevent a skin from forming.)

Scoop into bowls, sprinkle the ground *canela* on top, and serve.

SERVES 6 TO 8

NOTE: Some rices have a higher gluten content than others, making them thicken differently once cooled. If the rice thickens too much, simply stir in a little bit of milk. If you prefer a thinner rice pudding, use whole milk instead of cream.

Crepas de Cajeta | Crepes with Caramel-Pecan Sauce

Crepes

2 cups whole milk

4 eggs

5 tablespoons unsalted butter,
melted and cooled, plus extra for
cooking crepes

2 tablespoons sugar

½ teaspoon pure vanilla extract

½ teaspoon salt

¾ cup all-purpose flour

Caramel Sauce

2 tablespoons unsalted butter

3 cups *cajeta*, homemade
(page 151) or store-bought

1 cup whole goat's or cow's milk

¼ cup brandy or cognac

2 cups coarsely chopped,
toasted pecans

I believe I was about six years old when I fell in love for the first time. You see, Sundays are usually family days in Mexico, a day when brothers, sisters, aunts, uncles, cousins, grandparents, and parents stroll around and go out to eat. My parents would often take us to restaurants that had tableside service (but they were not as fancy as you might think), and my sister Yael and I always ordered the *crepas de cajeta*. They were only good if they were cooked as a spectacle, because that was a big part of the deliciousness that would soon follow. We would stand way too close to the waiter and impatiently watch as the butter bubbled when it hit the pan. The *cajeta* was poured and a thick, gooey caramel sauce slowly melted into a silky sheet that would cover and warm the golden crepes that were folded into triangles. We begged for the spoon that inevitably had some *cajeta* left on it, and more often than not had fights over it. And then we would take a step back so we could watch the blue and orange flames as if they were the "poof" in a magic trick. Oh, the anticipation would make our mouths water, and although we stood still, I felt as though my heart was jumping up and down every time—I thought they were palpitations for the man who made those wonderful crepes! We would rush to our seats as he plated the crepes and would hold our forks ready to attack. Yael always asked for vanilla ice cream, and it is the ideal complement to the dessert, even though, in my opinion, they are perfect just the way they are. If you would like them with ice cream, they go very nicely with Requesón Cheese Ice Cream (page 185).

TO MAKE THE CREPES, combine all the ingredients in a blender and blend until smooth. Refrigerate for 1 hour and blend again before using.

Heat a small nonstick pan (about 8 inches) over medium heat and brush lightly with butter. Ladle or pour about ¼ cup of the batter into it, tilting it all around to coat the bottom (the crepes should be thin but not completely see-through). Cook until the top is a nice golden color, flip carefully with a spatula, and cook until the second side is browned, 2 minutes total. Transfer to a plate and repeat to use up all the batter. When all the crepes are stacked up, separate them one by one and stack them again (this is to prevent sticking). The crepes can be made ahead of time and cooled, wrapped well in plastic, and frozen for up to 1 month. Let thaw before proceeding with the recipe.

CONTINUED

TO MAKE THE CARAMEL SAUCE, melt the butter in a large pan over medium heat until it begins to turn a slight brownish color and gives off a nutty aroma. Add the *cajeta* and milk and cook until bubbly and thickened, 3 to 5 minutes. Remove from the heat, add the brandy, and return to the heat, tilting the pan slightly to light the alcohol and burn it off (be careful). Add the crepes, one by one, submerging them in the sauce and folding them in half and then in half again so they look like triangles (alternatively, you can form the triangles beforehand and then submerge in the sauce or pour the sauce over them, but if you fold them once they are in the *cajeta*, you will ensure that they are evenly coated). Place about 3 on each plate and top with some of the toasted pecans.

SERVES ABOUT 8

4 cups goat's or cow's milk

1 cup sugar

1 tablespoon light corn syrup (optional)

¼ teaspoon salt

1 vanilla bean, split lengthwise, or 1 tablespoon pure vanilla extract, or 3 tablespoons brandy

¼ teaspoon baking soda, dissolved in 1 tablespoon cold water

Cajeta is another name for fruit pastes, or *ates*, and is a term still used in certain states, but the most familiar form of *cajeta* is the sweet caramel made from goat's or cow's milk and cooked down with sugar in copper pots. The goat's milk has a distinctive grassy, musky flavor and is the most commonly used for this application. The name derives from the wooden boxes called *cajetes* made from *tejamanil* or *ocote* (pine).

Adding a little corn syrup helps with the sticky consistency, but it can be left out if you prefer to make it the old-fashioned way. This luscious sauce is wonderful to top (warm) or swirl into ice cream, to accompany pancakes, or, better yet, to eat by the spoonful!

Combine the milk, sugar, corn syrup, and salt in a medium, tall, heavy-duty pot. Scrape the vanilla bean into the pot and add the pod (if using vanilla extract or brandy, do not add yet). Bring to a boil over medium heat, stirring occasionally so it doesn't stick to the bottom. Remove from the heat, add the baking soda, and stir carefully as it will bubble and steam up. When the bubbling has stopped, return it to the heat.

Adjust the heat so the mixture is at a constant simmer, stirring often so it doesn't stick to the bottom of the pan. Once it has turned a golden color, pay more attention and stir more often. Cook until it is thick and a dark caramel color, about 1 hour. (It will get thicker and stickier as it cools.) Remove from the heat. If using vanilla extract or brandy, add it now, being careful not to burn yourself because the *cajeta* may steam a little. Allow to cool before using. Remove the vanilla bean. (If you feel the caramel has thickened too much once it's cooled, simply stir in a bit of warm water).

MAKES 1 CUP

NOTE: Although it can't compare to the traditional made from scratch, a quick and easy way to make *cajeta* is with a can of condensed milk. Using a can opener, poke 2 to 3 holes in the top of the can, then place the can in a pot with simmering water for about 2 hours. (Make sure you don't forget the holes in the top—without them too much pressure can build up, causing the can to explode.) Open the can and add the vanilla or liquor. Pour out the *cajeta* and and store any leftover in a jar.

1 cup *cajeta*, homemade (page 151) or store-bought

Cake

¾ cup sugar

¾ cup all-purpose flour

⅓ cup unsweetened cocoa powder, preferably Dutch processed

½ teaspoon baking soda

¼ teaspoon baking powder

Pinch of salt

½ cup buttermilk

3 tablespoons vegetable oil

1 egg, at room temperature

½ teaspoon pure vanilla extract

Flan

1 (12-ounce) can evaporated milk

1 (14-ounce) can condensed milk

4 eggs

½ teaspoon pure vanilla extract

½ teaspoon salt

¾ cup coarsely chopped, toasted pecans or walnuts, for garnish

This dessert, also called *chocoflan*, gets its name from a magical thing that occurs in the oven. You cover the mold with some *cajeta*, pour in the chocolate cake batter, pour a layer of flan on top, and cover it lightly. It goes into the oven in a bigger dish with some hot water, and when you check whether it's done a little while later, you find that the flan is hidden somewhere and all you see is chocolate cake! You wait for it to cool, unmold it, and there is the flan! This is a sticky, rich, sweet dessert that is not for the faint of heart. Although you can make it in individual ramekins, there is something quite exciting about slicing a full-size one. It never ceases to amaze me.

Preheat the oven to 375°F. Lightly grease the bottom and sides of an 8-inch cake pan.

Pour the *cajeta* over the bottom and sides of the cake pan using a brush or the back of a spoon (you can heat the *cajeta* very slightly in the microwave so that it is easier to spread).

TO MAKE THE CAKE, combine the sugar, flour, cocoa powder, baking soda, baking powder, and salt in a large bowl and whisk until well blended. In a separate bowl, whisk together the buttermilk, vegetable oil, egg, and vanilla. Add to the flour mixture, whisking until thoroughly combined. Pour the cake batter into the pan and set aside.

TO MAKE THE FLAN, combine the evaporated milk, condensed milk, eggs, vanilla, and salt in a blender and blend until there are no visible lumps. Pour gently over the cake batter.

Cover loosely with foil, place in a large baking dish, and fill the baking dish with hot water so that it comes halfway up the sides. Bake until a toothpick inserted into the center comes out clean, about 50 minutes.

Remove the cake pan from the baking dish and allow to cool for at least 4 hours or refrigerate overnight. To unmold, lightly pass a warm knife around the edge, place a plate or dish on top, and carefully but rapidly flip over. Garnish with the toasted nuts. Serve cold or at room temperature.

SERVES 8 TO 10

Garabatos | Scribble Cookies

When I was a little girl, I would sneak downstairs with my cat Lider, while my sister and parents were asleep, and search the cupboard for the doily-lined tray that held these chocolate "sandwiches" decorated with an amusing chocolate scribble. I think these cookies were the first solid that my little brother ate.

Garabatos are still baked in the home of a lovely woman named Elvira Bleyer. She extended her home kitchen, attached a storefront to it, and named it Délvis. The bakery has expanded and is now a franchise. These cookies are not part of the traditional Mexican repertoire, but they are part of my culinary memory growing up in Mexico City and are still served for dessert. This version was developed through a collection of recipes from friends and colleagues, but mostly from palatable memory.

Preheat the oven to 350°F. Line 2 baking sheets with parchment paper.

TO MAKE THE COOKIES, place all the ingredients in a food processor and pulse until it starts coming together. Turn out onto a lightly floured surface and knead for a few minutes until you have a soft, uniform dough. Roll into a ball and flatten slightly with the palm of your hand. Roll out to about ¼ inch thick. With a cookie cutter or glass, cut out forty 2-inch circles (with straight or ridged edges) and place on the prepared baking sheets about ½ inch apart. (You can re-roll scraps up to 3 times, if necessary.)

Bake until firm to the touch and sightly brown around the edges (make sure they are still white in the center), 15 to 20 minutes. Allow to cool for a few minutes on the baking sheets, then transfer to a wire rack to cool completely.

TO MAKE THE FILLING, bring a saucepan of water to a simmer over low to medium heat. Place the chocolate in a metal bowl, set over the saucepan, making sure the water doesn't touch the bottom of the bowl, and cook, stirring often, until completely melted, 7 to 10 minutes.

Remove from the heat and set aside the saucepan with water. Add the butter, sour cream, corn syrup, and vanilla to the melted chocolate, and stir until well combined, being sure not to aerate the mixture. Place a small piece of plastic wrap directly on top of the mixture and let cool to room temperature.

TO MAKE THE TOPPING, return the saucepan of water to a simmer over low to medium heat. Combine the milk, confectioner's sugar, and chocolate in a metal bowl and set over the saucepan, making sure the water doesn't touch the bottom of the bowl, and cook, stirring often, until

Cookies

3 cups all-purpose flour

¾ cup confectioner's sugar

1 cup unsalted butter, cut into cubes, at room temperature

2 egg yolks

½ teaspoon pure vanilla extract

Chocolate Filling

5½ ounces semisweet chocolate, finely chopped

3½ tablespoons unsalted butter, softened

¼ cup sour cream

¼ cup light corn syrup

½ teaspoon pure vanilla extract

Topping

¼ cup whole milk

2½ tablespoons confectioner's sugar, sifted

3 ounces semisweet chocolate, finely chopped

2 ounces cocoa butter, finely chopped, or vegetable oil

completely melted, 5 to 7 minutes. Add the cocoa butter and continue cooking until a smooth glaze is formed, about 3 minutes. Keep warm.

Flip over 20 of the cookies. Using a piping bag fitted with a flat tip, or two spoons, spread about 1 tablespoon of filling on each of the flipped cookies. Place the remaining 20 cookies on top to make a sandwich and press down slightly to ensure the filling reaches the edges and is evenly spread.

Drizzle the warm chocolate topping over the cookies so that the top looks like a scribble. Let cool on a wire rack.

MAKES 20

NOTE: The filling and topping can be made ahead of time and refrigerated. Warm carefully in a microwave oven or water bath before using.

Chongos Zamoranos | Sweet Cinnamon Curds

I hesitated about including this recipe in the book because these sweet, cheeselike curds are quite unattractive and you might get scared away if this is the first recipe you try. There is no way around it, and even the most experienced photographer couldn't beautify them.

Once you get past their appearance, however, their wonderful, sweet cinnamony flavor comes through, and you will realize that the taste makes up for what they lack in the beauty department. They were originally created in the city of Zamora in Michoacán, but this recipe is derived from one prepared by the Esperanza clan at Dulcería Esperanza, a family-run candy business in another part of the same state that cooks more than 30 gallons of milk a day in huge rectangular copper pots to make them.

1 quart whole milk

¾ cup sugar

1 tablespoon freshly squeezed lemon juice

6 drops liquid rennet, or 1 tablet rennet

4 (3-inch) pieces *canela*

Combine the milk and sugar in a large pot and cook over medium heat, stirring, until the sugar dissolves (don't let it come to a boil). Add the lemon juice. Remove from the heat, add the rennet drops (if you're using the rennet tablet, dissolve in a bit of cold milk before adding), and allow to set up, about 30 minutes.

While the curds are still in the pot, carefully cut them into squares about 3 by 3 inches, tuck the *canela* between a few of the squares, and cook over very low heat (it should never come to a boil) until the cubes turn a slight yellowish color and the syrup has thickened, about 2 hours.

Remove the squares carefully with a slotted spoon, transfer to a serving platter, place the *canela* on top, and strain the syrup over it. Serve at room temperature or chilled.

SERVES 8

Buñuelos | Thin Cinnamon-Sugar Fritters

4 tomatillo husks

⅔ cup water

½ teaspoon *tequesquite*

4 cups all-purpose flour, sifted

½ teaspoon baking powder

Pinch of salt

¼ cup freshly squeezed orange juice

1 egg

1 tablespoon sugar

1 cup lard or unsalted butter, at room temperature, plus a little extra

½ cup whole milk

1 cup sugar mixed with 1 tablespoon freshly ground *canela*, for rolling, or about 1 cup *piloncillo* syrup, for serving

Oil, for frying (about 4 cups)

These fritters are often referred to as *buñuelos de rodilla*, or knee fritters, as they need to be quite thin and the knee is often pressed into the dough to stretch it out. Christmas is the best time to look for them; if you're lucky, you will find a street stand with enormous *buñuelos* piled up high and fried to order.

My friend Valeria's mom is famous for her *buñuelos*. She starts preparing them in mid-October to be able to have enough fritters to fill the countless baskets she sends as Christmas gifts. I am fortunate that she was kind enough to show me how to make these incredibly crispy and tasty *buñuelos*. She makes the dough by hand and has her own unique way of kneading it; however, I chose to do it in a machine to make it easier for those of us who haven't been making them for two decades.

Tequesquite is mineral lime and an alkaline (like baking soda) that is used to help the *buñuelos* puff up. You can find it in many specialty Latin and Mexican markets or at some spice specialty shops (see Sources).

Combine the tomatillo husks, water, and *tequesquite* in a saucepan over medium heat and bring to a boil. Remove from the heat, let cool, and strain. Reserve the liquid and discard the rest.

Combine the flour, baking powder, and salt in a mixer with the hook attachment. Add the orange juice, egg, sugar, tomatillo husk infusion, lard, and milk. Beat until the dough is very smooth and elastic, 15 to 20 minutes. Rub some of the lard all over the top of the dough and cover lightly with a cloth. Allow to rest, at room temperature, for at least 30 minutes.

Cover a table with a clean sheet or tablecloth. Grease your hands with a little lard and divide the dough into 18 golf ball–size pieces. Roll each into a smooth ball, pressing so they're compact. Cover them lightly with a cloth. Roll each ball into a circle about 5 inches in diameter, turning as you roll, so that it is even.

Beginning with the ones that were rolled out first, stretch each circle, pulling very gently from the center and around the edges, to form a circle 8 to 9 inches in diameter. You should be able to see through the dough.

Allow the *buñuelos* to rest over the tablecloth until they feel dry to the touch and look a bit leathery, 20 to 25 minutes. Turn them over and let dry completely on the other side, 15 to 20 minutes.

CONTINUED

Spread the sugar-*canela* mixture on a plate and place a wire rack over a baking sheet for draining. (A wire rack with only one row of metal spacers instead of a crisscross pattern works best, as you can drain the *buñuelos* vertically.)

Pour the oil into a deep-sided pan to a depth of at least 3 inches. Heat the oil to 375°F over medium heat, slide a *buñuelo* very carefully into the oil, and press down with a fork. The *buñuelo* should immediately begin to bubble around the edges and blister all over. Fry until golden on one side, then flip over and fry until golden on the other side, 1 to 2 minutes total. Remove the *buñuelo* from the oil, let the excess oil drip back into the pot for a few seconds, then place on the wire rack to drain. Fry the remaining *buñuelos* in the same manner.

Toss the *buñuelos* in the sugar-*canela* mixture while still warm or serve with *piloncillo* syrup.

MAKES 18 TO 24

VARIATIONS:
BUÑUELOS POBRES AND BUÑUELOS AHOGADOS

Buñuelos pobres are lightly coated with anise-flavored syrup, and *buñuelos ahogados* are submerged in warm *piloncillo* syrup (page 190) and topped with colored sugar or sprinkles.

Niño Envuelto de Merengue con Fresas y Crema | Strawberry Meringue Cake Roll

Niño envuelto means "wrapped baby," and it is basically a sponge cake filled with some kind of jam, cream, *cajeta*, or mousse, rolled up tightly, and covered with confectioner's sugar, cream, coconut, almonds, chocolate, or meringue. It is served as a dessert, but you can also find it in *panaderías* sold in slices.

Although I have always loved sweets, cake has never been my favorite dessert, and I think it's because I really like crunchy things. The one exception to this rule is *pastel de fresas con crema* (vanilla cake filled and covered with whipped cream and strawberries). When I think about this cake, my mouth waters and I remember the Gran Via bakery, which has been making one of the best versions of this cake since the late 1960s. When the bakery first started, they sold only two things: this strawberry layered cake and huge meringues filled with whipped cream. So, when deciding what kind of *niño envuelto* to make, it seemed only natural to blend all of these flavors and textures into one.

It is important that the eggs be at room temperature to ensure a spongy cake, so separate the eggs, cover them, and allow to come to room temperature for 30 minutes before whipping.

Preheat the oven to 350°F. Grease 2 baking sheets and line with parchment paper. Reserve one of the prepared baking sheets for the meringue and lightly grease and flour the parchment paper of the one you will use for the cake.

TO MAKE THE CAKE, in a bowl, beat the egg yolks with the granulated sugar and salt until thick and pale, about 5 minutes. Add the vanilla. In a separate bowl, whip the egg whites until they are stiff, but not dry, 4 to 6 minutes. Carefully fold the egg whites into the egg-yolk mixture. Sprinkle a little bit of the sifted flour on top, fold in carefully, and repeat, gradually adding the rest of the flour. Spread the batter evenly on the prepared pan using an offset spatula.

Bake until the cake is golden and springs back when lightly pressed in the center, 15 to 20 minutes. Remove the cake from the oven and let cool. Decrease the oven temperature to 275°F. Once the cake has cooled slightly, run a knife around the edges, put a piece of parchment paper on top, flip it over, remove the parchment paper from the bottom, and leave bottom side up to spread the filling.

TO MAKE THE MERINGUE, make sure your bowl is very clean and very dry. Beat the egg whites with the salt until it is bubbly and beginning to thicken but has not quite reached soft peaks. Gradually

Cake

8 egg yolks, at room temperature

⅔ cup granulated sugar

¼ teaspoon salt

½ teaspoon pure vanilla extract

4 egg whites, at room temperature

⅔ cup all-purpose flour, sifted

Meringue

4 egg whites, at room temperature

Pinch of salt

1 cup granulated sugar

Filling

1½ cups heavy cream

⅓ cup confectioner's sugar

½ vanilla bean, scraped, or 1½ teaspoons pure vanilla extract

2½ to 3 cups sliced or chopped strawberries

add the granulated sugar while still beating, and continue to beat until stiff but not dry peaks form, 3 to 5 minutes.

Spoon the meringue into a piping bag fitted with a tip attachment or into a plastic bag with the corner cut off. Pipe strips 4 to 6 inches long onto the reserved baking sheet. Bake until dry, 15 to 20 minutes. Let cool. Crush slightly, if desired.

TO MAKE THE FILLING, beat the heavy cream with an electric mixer or by hand until slightly thickened. Add the confectioner's sugar and vanilla and continue beating until thick and smooth, 5 to 7 minutes total.

You are now ready to assemble the cake. Make sure that you leave a little bit of filling, strawberries, and plenty of meringue for topping. Spread some of the filling all over the cake, sprinkle on some of the crushed meringue, and top with a layer of strawberries. Roll tightly away from you, tuck the seam under the roll, cover with the remaining filling, and decorate with the remaining strawberries. Freeze for 15 minutes or refrigerate for 30 minutes (don't refrigerate it for longer than 1 hour or the meringue will lose its crunch). Top with the remaining meringue, decorating as you wish. Serve immediately (as if you could resist the temptation!).

SERVES 8 TO 10

Capirotada de Guayaba con Plátano | Banana-Guava Bread Pudding

Capirotada is Mexico's version of bread pudding and is traditionally served during *Semana Santa* (Lent). It is made with day-old crusty bread that is lightly fried and layered or topped with various ingredients, such as raisins, peanuts, coconut, tomato, or cheese, and baked with sweetened milk or *piloncillo* syrup.

I had the good fortune to stumble upon this incredible bread pudding in Tlaxcala. Cecilia and I met through my dad and immediately sparked a friendship. She told me her mom's recipe was the best *capirotada* ever and that it had to be in the book. She was so right! I visited her mother's home, where I stayed and cooked for a few days. I had never met her before but was warmly welcomed by her with kindness and sweetness. The day after we prepared this unusual bread pudding (originally from Jalisco), the sweet aroma of fragrant guavas and *piloncillo* lingered in the air as we enjoyed a slice for breakfast with a delicious glass of cold raw milk.

6 cups water

10 ounces *piloncillo*, chopped, or 1 cup firmly packed dark brown sugar plus 1½ tablespoons molasses

1 5-inch piece *canela*

2 whole cloves

1½ pounds fresh guavas

1-pound loaf day-old baguette

2 to 4 tablespoons vegetable oil

3 tablespoons lard or unsalted butter

6 (6-inch) corn tortillas

⅓ cup dark raisins

⅓ cup coarsely chopped pecans

2 bananas, cut into ½-inch-thick slices

8 ounces Munster or Monterey Jack cheese, shredded

Combine the water, *piloncillo*, *canela*, and cloves in a large pot and cook over medium heat until the *piloncillo* has dissolved, 7 to 10 minutes. Wash the guavas and cut off the ends. Cut into ¼-inch-thick slices and add, seeds and all, to the hot liquid. Cook at a soft simmer until the guavas are fork-tender, about 20 minutes. Remove the guavas from the syrup with a slotted spoon and let sit until cool enough to handle. Continue cooking the liquid over medium heat until thickened to the consistency of maple syrup, 20 to 30 minutes.

Slice the ends off the baguette and cut the remaining bread into ½-inch-thick slices. Warm a large skillet over medium heat, swirl in a little bit of the oil to coat, and, working in batches, brown the bread slices on both sides. Wipe the pan between each use and use only enough oil so the bread doesn't stick (it shouldn't be oily at all).

Remove the seeds from the guavas using your hands or a spoon. Press the seeds and any liquid through a colander into the syrup, and then strain the syrup.

Preheat the oven to 350°F. Grease a deep 2½-quart baking dish with a bit of the lard, spreading it with one of the tortillas, and then layer the bottom and sides of the dish with the tortillas. Whisk the remaining lard into the syrup.

Layer half of the bread slices in the dish and top with half of the guava slices, raisins, pecans, banana slices, and cheese. Pour about 1 cup of the syrup over all. Layer the remaining bread on top and scatter the remaining guava slices, raisins, pecans, banana slices, and cheese all over the top. Pour the remaining syrup over all, cover loosely with aluminum foil, and bake until the syrup has been absorbed, 50 to 60 minutes. Allow to cool for at least 30 minutes before serving.

SERVES 8 TO 10

Natilla | Sweet Custard Sauce

3 cups whole milk

2 long strips lime zest

1 (3- to 4-inch) piece *canela*

4 egg yolks

1 cup heavy cream

½ cup sugar

3 tablespoons cornstarch

¼ teaspoon salt

Freshly ground *canela*, for sprinkling

This custard is a very tasty dessert and is often served with fruit, cookies, or pound cake. Although it is called a sauce, the *natilla* takes center stage rather than the other way around. Many convents serve it in a large bowl and dust freshly ground *canela* over a stencil to create a religious symbol or figure on top. I particularly like it with fruit such as mango, guava, or berries.

Combine the milk, lime zest, and *canela* in a saucepan and cook over medium heat until bubbles form around the edges, 3 to 5 minutes. Meanwhile, combine the egg yolks, heavy cream, sugar, cornstarch, and salt in a large heatproof bowl and whisk until the cornstarch has dissolved and there are no lumps.

Put the bowl on a towel so it doesn't move around. Gradually whisk half of the hot milk mixture into the egg-yolk mixture, then carefully return everything to the saucepan. Continue cooking, stirring often, until it coats the back of a spoon.

Strain the mixture and chill over an ice bath. Place a piece of plastic wrap directly on top so it doesn't form a crust. When ready to serve, sprinkle some ground *canela* on top, and enjoy.

SERVES 6

Milhojas de Crema con Mango y Coco | Pastry Cream Napoleon with Mango and Coconut

Milhojas, or "thousand leaves," is the name given to this pastry because, just as in the fall, when the autumn leaves trickle down and move as the wind blows, tiny pieces of this crunchy, flaky pastry fly around when you take a bite of it. This recipe is one example where the French influence in Mexico began to be very apparent during the rule of Porfirio Díaz at the beginning of the twentieth century, and a love for classic French pastries has remained part of our tradition ever since.

Milhojas have remained a favorite dessert and are found all over Mexico in many pastry shops and bread bakeries. As with many other desserts, they are often sold by the slice. Although *milhojas* are often filled with jams, mousses, and whipped cream, this one is layered with pastry cream, which I find to be the most representative one of all. The addition of mangoes and coconut gives it a nice freshness and tropical flavor.

Traditional puff pastry is a bit time-consuming to prepare, so I have provided a quick "mock" version that will work very well when you don't have the time or patience required to make the real deal.

TO MAKE THE QUICK PUFF PASTRY, combine the flour and salt in a medium-size bowl. Blend the butter into the flour mixture with a pastry blender or a food processor until it resembles coarse meal. Add about 4 ounces of the water and mix until it just comes together. Add a little more of the remaining water if needed, but don't overmix. Flatten into a disk, wrap in plastic, and refrigerate for at least 30 minutes.

Turn the dough out onto a lightly floured surface and roll into an 18 by 15-inch rectangle about ½ inch thick, making sure the edges are smooth and straight. Turn the rectangle so that the longest side is closest to you. Fold both sides into the center and then fold in half like a book. Turn the dough 90 degrees and roll again into a rectangle of the same size as before. Fold the same way as before, wrap in plastic, and refrigerate for 1 hour.

Preheat the oven to 350°F. Lightly grease a baking sheet.

Turn the dough out onto a lightly floured surface and roll into a rectangle the size of your baking sheet. Cut lengthwise into 3 even pieces. Transfer to the prepared baking sheet. Bake until the pastry is golden all over, 20 to 25 minutes, remove from the oven, and increase the oven temperature to 400°F. Dust some sifted confectioner's sugar all over the top and bake until the sugar melts and looks caramelized, 3 to 5 minutes. This will make the pastry a little crunchier and will form a shield so that the cream won't make it soggy as quickly.

Quick Puff Pastry

3 cups all-purpose flour

1½ teaspoons sea salt

1⅔ cups cold unsalted butter, cut into small pieces

5 to 6 ounces ice-cold water

Sifted confectioner's sugar, for dusting

Pastry Cream

2 cups whole milk

1 vanilla bean, halved lengthwise and scraped

5 egg yolks

½ cup granulated sugar

¼ cup cornstarch

1½ tablespoons unsalted butter

Whipped Cream

1 cup heavy cream

¼ cup confectioner's sugar

½ teaspoon pure vanilla extract

1 or 2 ripe mangoes, cut into slices or cubes

1 cup unsweetened flaked coconut, toasted

TO MAKE THE PASTRY CREAM, combine the milk, scraped vanilla bean, and pod in a saucepan and bring to a boil over medium heat. Meanwhile, combine the egg yolks, granulated sugar, and cornstarch in a heatproof bowl. Gradually whisk half of the hot milk mixture into the egg-yolk mixture, then carefully return everything to the saucepan. Continue whisking over medium heat until thick and bubbly, 1 to 2 minutes. Remove from the heat, whisk in the butter, and remove and discard the vanilla pod. Pour into a heatproof bowl and place plastic wrap directly on top. Let chill completely in the refrigerator (the pastry cream can be made up to 2 days in advance and simply needs to be whisked well before using).

TO MAKE THE WHIPPED CREAM, beat the heavy cream with an electric mixer or by hand until slightly thickened. Add the confectioner's sugar and vanilla and continue beating until thickened but not stiff, 5 to 7 minutes. Fold the whipped cream into the chilled pastry cream until well blended. Transfer 1 cup of the mixture to a separate bowl and reserve.

Turn a baking sheet upside down, place one pastry layer on top, carefully spread half of the remaining cream mixture all over, place another pastry layer on top, and press down gently. Spread the remaining cream mixture on top. Arrange the mango slices on top of the cream and finish with the remaining pastry layer. Press down gently. Cover the sides with the reserved cream mixture, smoothing it out while tilting the pan slightly and carefully, then sprinkle all over with the toasted coconut. If desired, dust with confectioner's sugar in 1-inch diagonal lines (make a quick stencil out of cardboard or plastic). Refrigerate for 30 to 45 minutes before slicing and serving.

SERVES 8 TO 10

Calabaza en Tacha | Candied Pumpkin

2 oranges

1½ pounds chopped *piloncillo*, or 1½ cups firmly packed dark brown sugar mixed with 2 tablespoons molasses

3 (5-inch) pieces *canela*

6 whole cloves

4 cups water

1 (4- to 5-pound) pumpkin

Although pumpkin is not technically a fruit, it is eaten in this sweet preparation, as many fruits are. There are many foods specially made for Día de los Muertos celebrations throughout Mexico, and this is one of the most representative. It is traditionally cooked in clay casseroles, with the seeds and strands attached, but you can also clean and dry the seeds and snack on them later.

Remove the orange zest (no white part) from the oranges with a peeler and place in a pot. Squeeze in the juice, then add the *piloncillo*, *canela*, cloves, and water. Cook over medium heat, stirring occasionally, until the *piloncillo* has dissolved, 5 to 10 minutes.

Meanwhile, cut the stem off the pumpkin and cut it in half lengthwise (scraping out the seeds and strings if you want to use them for something else or simply don't want them in the dish). Cut each piece in half lengthwise again, and then cut each piece in half widthwise so you have wedges 2 to 3 inches wide. Place a layer of pumpkin, flesh side down, in a pot and then place the next layers flesh side up. Cover with the syrup and cook at a soft simmer over medium heat until the pumpkin is tender and the syrup has thickened, is dark brown, and looks like a glaze, about 2 hours. Serve at room temperature or chilled.

SERVES 8

DELICIAS HELADAS

FROZEN TREATS

SOME YEARS AGO, my aunt Alex told me about an ice cream town she had heard about, and we quickly made plans to go there. We had only a general idea of where it was, with no name or main reference. After getting lost numerous times, we found ourselves in a small town on the outskirts of Mexico City. On one side of the main street were about fifteen ice cream vendors lined up side by side. Hand-cranked ice cream *garrafas* made of wood and metal sat on a bed of ice inside colorful handpainted wooden buckets.

How to decide which one to try? They all looked the same. We stared at the fluorescent cardboard signs listing ice cream flavors called "sigh of an angel," "moon's lullaby," "mermaid's song," "drunk cream," "lover's melody," and "devil's kiss." We didn't know what these names meant, but we knew we were in a magical place. A knock on the car window startled us. Mariano, a skinny kid about ten years old, told us, "I know you're sitting here wondering where to go, and let me assure you that our ice cream is the best." He explained that he made the ice cream every morning with his father and that his mother taught him when the fruits were ripe enough to be picked from the fields behind their house and how to milk the cows from which the cream was made.

We ordered our first ice cream by choosing from the poetic names. Each stand had between ten and fifteen flavors. My sister Yael's "red awakening" was a red tuna fruit sorbet. I had a *tres leches* ice cream sweetened with lightly caramelized goat's milk and finished with a little sour cream.

We tried a couple more flavors and proceeded to other stands to be fair. Our next vendor, Fernando, was Mariano's uncle. They shared the cow, but not their recipes. He served us pecan ice cream, which had a deep, toasty flavor, and guava sorbet, made from fruits picked just the day before. From other stands we tried corn with *queso fresco*, *zapote* with tangerine, piquín chile,

fig with mezcal, and amaranth with honey. By the time we headed back to our car we had tried at least fifteen flavors. We were giddy and filled with joy. I've never been able to find that exact place again (I'm still searching), but I know it wasn't a dream because I wasn't alone.

The fact remains, though, that there is an incredible array of frozen treats in Mexico, and they have a fascinating history—a struggle of sorts. Oral tradition tells of the Aztecs gathering ice and snow from the top of the Iztaccíhuatl and Popocatépetl volcanoes in central Mexico to preserve food for the emperors.

The Spaniards had many more places from which they could collect ice for their different needs, but when they arrived in Mexico their options were limited to these volcanoes. It was also much more complicated to gather because of the high altitude. Therefore, the Spanish implemented rules that affected the majority of the population but benefited only themselves. They established monopolies to make some products the exclusive property of the throne, including silk, salt, gunpowder, and ice. They didn't collect or distribute the ice or snow themselves, but would sell the right to do so to the highest bidder. That person was the only one allowed to collect them from the mountains and sell them to the public. That person was also the only one allowed to sell frozen treats of any kind, and he had to pay an annual fee to do so.

The response to this monopoly gave rise to a black market of ice and snow and clandestine frozen preparations that were hard to monitor and control. It amazes me that not only did this system not deter people from concocting frozen treats, but it also led to a culinary tradition that has been passed on from generation to generation.

Making commercial frozen treats for the black market was no easy task, though. The vendors would hire someone to gather ice in metal buckets, which were then wrapped in a wet cloth, placed inside a sack filled with ice, and transported by donkeys. The service needed to be fast and efficient and done very early in the morning so that the ice cream maker would have time to freeze the treats. In addition, weather made the enterprise unpredictable and unreliable.

The most important medium of commercialization of frozen treats was through a sort of primitive *nevería* (ice cream shop) called an *estanquillo*. These *estanquillos* would prepare, freeze, and sell ice creams, sorbets, and blocks of ice. They did not have a shop or a place of business, but rather would be hired for special occasions and festivities. The treats were exclusive to the upper classes because of the high cost of production.

In 1823, the monopoly was lifted and frozen treats spread to the masses. They were made and sold primarily in two ways: the artisanal way, where ice cream was made daily and sold at fairs, on streets, and in parks, and the European model of the coffee shop, where ice cream was enjoyed at tables indoors and along sidewalks. The popularization of frozen treats became a bridge between social classes.

In 1884, the Feria de la Nieve was held in the town of Tulyehualco, and it still takes place to this day, offering flavors such as rattlesnake, mole, pork skin, and *tepache* (a fermented pineapple drink). This festival is often referred to as the "Fair of the 1,000 Flavors."

Ice cream cones and ice pops were introduced at the beginning of the twentieth century, and the influence of the United States between 1920 and 1930 brought banana splits, hot fudge sundaes, ice cream floats, and eskimo pies. Mexticacán, in Jalisco, and Tocumbo, in Michoacán, are places immediately identified with Popsicle-style frozen treats. But in Mexico, these are not just sticks of unnatural colors and artificial flavors. They encapsulate the wonderfully colorful, ripe fruit that abounds, and the selection is quite incredible. The *paletas*, or ice pops, are often scented with flower petals, enriched with buttery pecans or spiced with chile, and studded with ripe chunks of fruit.

Frozen sweets are not limited to ice creams, sorbets, and *paletas*, however. The array is enormous and mostly apparent as you travel south, were the warm climate has inspired many specialties. Veracruz has its *glorias*—mashed banana mixed with vanilla and topped with shaved ice, condensed milk, sweet grenadine syrup, and cinnamon. The *diablitos de chamoy* from southeastern Mexico make a salty-sour-sweet concoction of fermented stone fruits, finely shaved ice, and ripe local fruits.

No matter where you are in Mexico, there will be a plaza, a shop, a cart, a street stand, a restaurant, or even an undiscovered ice cream town that will help you cool off in a tasty way and surprise you with an incredible variety of flavors and textures.

Nieve de Membrillo | Quince Sorbet

Whenever I visit Pátzcuaro, Michoacán, I always look forward to the ice creams in the main square. During my last visit, as I waited for the crowds to diminish at noontime so that I could interview Amparo Contreras de Galván with my childhood friend Martha Silva, I had a couple of scoops of sorbet. I tend to order the same ones wherever I go, but the *membrillo* one at La Pancada caught my eye. As I took a bite, without even swallowing it, I knew it had to be in the book. Although the famous ice creams in the town are called *pastes*, I have to say, this was the one for me. Whenever something so special comes my way, I remember it vividly, taking mental notes of each layer of flavor and texture that at times allows me to re-create things I love so much.

I must say, this quince sorbet is pretty close to the one I had. I suggest you make a batch of the Requesón Cheese Ice Cream (page 185) to go with it, in the classic pairing of cheese and quince but in a whole new way.

Peel, quarter, and core the quinces. Put into a pot with the cider, sugar, and salt and cook over medium heat, uncovered, until very tender, about 30 minutes, making sure the mixture never boils but is always at a simmer.

Let cool for about 30 minutes, then purée in a blender until smooth. Strain and cool over an ice bath. Refrigerate, covered, until completely chilled, 2 to 3 hours. Freeze in an ice cream maker according to the manufacturer's instructions.

MAKES ABOUT 1 QUART

1½ pounds ripe quinces (about 4)

5 cups unsweetened apple cider

¾ cup sugar

Pinch of salt

Nieve de Pepino | Cucumber Sorbet

Sliced cucumbers mixed with salt, lime, and chile are often eaten in Mexico as a snack and are even sold at movie theaters. I was about thirteen when I first tried this combination as a sorbet on a warm day in Cuernavaca. Well, this time the flavor of the cucumber was heightened with a little sugar, and the sorbet was topped with a mixture of chile and lime.

I've included the chiles in the sorbet itself, by infusing them in the syrup; however, you can always sprinkle some powdered chile on top after it has set.

½ cup sugar

½ cup water

2 whole arbol chiles (optional)

2 large seedless English cucumbers, washed, unpeeled, coarsely chopped

Juice of ½ lemon

Juice of 1 lime

¼ teaspoon salt

2 egg whites

Combine the sugar, water, and chiles in a small pot and cook over medium heat, stirring, until the sugar has dissolved. Allow to cool slightly, then add the cucumbers, lemon juice, lime juice, and salt. Transfer to a blender and purée until smooth. Strain through a fine-mesh sieve, pressing down with a wooden spoon to extract as much juice as possible. Whisk the egg whites until frothy and fold into the cucumber mixture.

Cool over an ice bath. Refrigerate, covered, until completely chilled, 2 hours. Freeze in an ice cream maker according to the manufacturer's instructions.

MAKES 3 TO 3½ CUPS

Nieve de Chabacano | Apricot Sorbet

1½ pounds ripe apricots

1 cup water

¾ cup sugar

Pinch of salt

1 tablespoon freshly squeezed lemon or lime juice

Whenever I crave a cold sweet treat, I always go for the *nieves*. Ice cream is great, of course, but I am all about the fruit. Anyone who knows me knows that I can eat a quarter of a watermelon in half an hour, that I eat six to ten pieces of fruit per day during the summer, and that I have a particular weakness for stone fruit. The fruit is always the main focus in sorbet, with no distractions.

Although the variety of stone fruit is not as diverse in Mexico as it is in other parts of the world, we have some tart and sweet apricots that make an extremely refreshing and silky *nieve*. Feel free to substitute any other stone fruit that is ripe and in season.

Wash the apricots and cut into quarters, discarding the pits. Combine with the water and sugar in a pot and cook over medium heat, without letting it boil, until the apricots are tender, 10 to 15 minutes.

Let cool for about 30 minutes, then purée in a blender. Add the salt and lemon juice and blend until smooth. Strain and cool over an ice bath. Refrigerate, covered, until completely chilled, about 2 hours. Freeze in an ice cream maker according to the manufacturer's instructions.

MAKES ABOUT 3 CUPS

Nieve de Limón Oaxaqueño | Oaxaca-Style Lime Sorbet

If you've ever visited Oaxaca, my favorite state in all of Mexico, undoubtedly you have seen people walking around with cones or cups filled with fluorescent green sorbet. I try to stay away from colorings, especially when it comes to fruit preparations, but if you can get past the scary color, you'll discover a surprisingly refreshing flavor. The color may not be subtle, but the flavor is, and lime is one of the most popular flavors in Oaxaca.

Try to select very green small limes, because they tend to have the best flavor. Be sure to wash and dry them very well. Although the original recipe doesn't call for fresh lime juice, I find that a little bit balances the sweetness of the sorbet and adds another layer of flavor.

6 limes (preferably unwaxed)

3¾ cups water

1 cup sugar

¼ cup freshly squeezed lime juice (from about 3 limes)

Zest the limes, making sure you get only the green part, and mix half of it with 3 cups of the water. Refrigerate for 1 hour to extract the flavor.

In a saucepan, combine the remaining ¾ cup water, the sugar, and the remaining zest and bring to a soft boil over medium heat until the sugar dissolves. Continue cooking for a couple of minutes so that it thickens slightly. Remove from the heat, let cool, and then strain through a fine-mesh sieve.

Put a cheesecloth-lined sieve over a bowl and strain the lime-flavored water. Add the syrup and the lime juice to the bowl and stir gently. Chill over an ice bath, stirring, until cool. Refrigerate, covered, until completely cool, about 2 hours, and freeze in an ice cream maker according to the manufacturer's instructions.

MAKES ABOUT 1 QUART

Nieve de Tamarindo | Tamarind Sorbet

Tamarind, a tropical fruit native to Asia, looks sort of like a brown fava bean with a hard tan shell that surrounds a sticky, meaty brown flesh. The fruit is often mixed with chile, and I found more than three dozen different candies made from it. Tamarind sorbet has a seductive tartness that comes through in this smooth *nieve*.

10 ounces unpeeled tamarinds, or 8 ounces tamarind pulp with seeds

4 cups water

1½ cups sugar

Remove the outer hard shell from the tamarinds and discard the "strings" that are attached to the flesh. Place the tamarind flesh or pulp in a pot, cover with the water, and bring to a boil over medium heat. Adjust the heat to maintain a constant simmer and cook, stirring occasionally, until tender, 30 to 40 minutes. Let sit until cool enough to handle.

Strain through a fine-mesh sieve (don't wash the sieve just yet because you'll be using it for the pulp) and measure the liquid. Add enough water to make 4 cups. Return the liquid to the pot, add the sugar, and cook over medium heat until the sugar dissolves (don't let the mixture come to a boil). Remove from the heat.

Press the pulp through the sieve with your hand, a spoon, or a spatula to extract as much as possible. Discard the seeds and add the pulp to the pot. Stir to combine. Chill over an ice bath until cool. Refrigerate, covered, until completely cool, about 2 hours, and freeze in an ice cream maker according to the manufacturer's instructions.

MAKES ABOUT 5 CUPS

Paletas de Nuez | Pecan Ice Pops

1 cup coarsely chopped toasted pecans

1 cup heavy cream

1 cup whole milk

⅔ cup sugar

Pinch of salt

1 teaspoon pure vanilla extract

This is a very simple frozen dessert with an intense pecan flavor. Many of the ice creams and pops in Mexico have a pleasant grainy texture, and in this case it is produced by puréeing only a portion of the steeped nuts, so be sure to use high-quality, fresh nuts.

Combine the pecans, heavy cream, milk, sugar, and salt in a heavy pot and bring to a boil over medium heat. Remove from the heat, add the vanilla, cover, and let sit for 30 minutes. Remove 1 cup of the mixture, purée in a blender, then return to the pot and stir to combine.

Chill over an ice bath, stirring until cool. Refrigerate until completely cooled. Divide the mixture among ice pop molds or wax-lined paper cups and freeze until beginning to set, 3 to 4 hours. Insert the sticks. Let freeze for at least 3 hours more, and then unmold as directed or peel off the paper cups.

MAKES 8 TO 10

Paletas de Mango Enchilado | Spicy Mango Ice Pops

¾ cup sugar

¾ cup water

2 dried arbol chiles, with seeds, broken into pieces

2½ cups fresh mango purée

3 small limes, juiced

1 to 2 medium mangoes, diced

½ to ¾ cup ground piquín or other chile powder (depending on how spicy you want them)

My brother Pedro loves anything with mango and chile, and he's not alone. It has become one of the most common combinations in sweets in Mexico; in fact, when you eat fresh mango, powdered chile of some kind is always on the table. I wanted to do something in this book just for him, but I am sure he won't mind sharing (that's the kind of guy he is).

The chile powder you use is a matter of taste. It isn't just about the heat; it's also about the flavor. I particularly like the piquín chile from Oaxaca, but feel free to substitute it for ground guajillo, chipotle, or your personal favorite.

Combine the sugar, water, and chile pieces in a small pot and cook over medium heat, stirring, until the sugar has dissolved. Remove from the heat, allow to cool, and strain. Stir in the mango purée and the lime juice. In a medium bowl, toss together the mango pieces with the chile powder.

Divide the chile-coated mango chunks among ice pop molds or wax-lined paper cups, then pour the mango purée mixture over the top. Freeze until beginning to set, 3 to 4 hours. Insert the sticks. Let freeze for at least 3 hours more, and then unmold as directed or peel off the paper cups.

If you prefer to use the chile powder on the outside, unmold the pops and allow to thaw slightly (so the chile powder will stick to it), place the chile powder in a shallow bowl, then dip the pops in to coat.

MAKES 6 TO 8

Paletas de Jamaica | Hibiscus Ice Pops

1½ cups hibiscus flowers

6 cups water

¾ cup sugar

The bright burgundy color of the hibiscus is only half the beauty of this delicious flower. It is one of the most common flavors for *aguas frescas*, and its acidity is fantastic in this yummy frozen treat.

Combine all the ingredients in a pot and bring to a boil over medium heat. Reduce the heat to a simmer and continue cooking until reduced by half to 3 cups liquid, 20 to 30 minutes. Remove from the heat and allow to steep for 30 minutes. Strain through a fine-mesh sieve (if it reduced too much, simply add a little hot water).

CONTINUED

Chill over an ice bath, stirring until cool. Refrigerate until completely cooled. Divide the mixture among ice pop molds or wax-lined paper cups and freeze until beginning to set, 3 to 4 hours. Insert the sticks. Let freeze for at least 3 more hours, and then unmold as directed or peel off the paper cups.

MAKES 6 TO 8

Raspado de Margarita | Margarita Ice

Who doesn't love a margarita? Well, this is one way to get the flavor in a very refreshing ice that you can keep on hand in your freezer. You'll be tempted to add more tequila, but try to refrain, because it won't freeze.

Combine the water, sugar, and lime zest in a small pot and cook over medium heat, stirring, until the sugar has dissolved. Remove from the heat, allow to cool, and strain. Add the tequila, lime juice, orange liqueur, and salt. Mix well and pour into a shallow pan.

Put in the freezer and check on it in about 1 hour. Once the edges start to freeze, scrape lightly with a fork and continue freezing. Check the ice every hour, scraping with a fork each time, until completely frozen. If the ice crystals are too large, leave at room temperature for 15 to 20 minutes, or until it begins to melt again, and then freeze as before.

MAKES 1 QUART

2½ cups water

¾ cup sugar

Zest of 1 lime

3 tablespoons white tequila

½ cup freshly squeezed lime juice

1 tablespoon orange liqueur

Pinch of salt

Raspado de Mandarina | Tangerine Ice

4 cups freshly squeezed
tangerine juice

¾ cup sugar

1 teaspoon freshly squeezed
lime juice

½ teaspoon salt

Raspados are sold by street hawkers, particularly in warm climates, where they are especially refreshing. The vendors pour colorful sweet syrups over shaved ice, and the flavors vary depending on which fruits grow locally (although some vendors use artificial flavors).

This tangerine ice has a naturally refreshing fruitiness. You can substitute any other citrus, or combination of citrus, and can add up to 1 cup of sugar if the fruit is tart.

Combine 1 cup of the tangerine juice with the sugar in a small pot and cook over medium heat, stirring, until the sugar has dissolved. Remove from the heat and add the remaining 3 cups tangerine juice, the lime juice, and the salt. Mix well and pour into a shallow pan.

Put in the freezer and check on it in about 1 hour. Once the edges start to freeze, scrape lightly with a fork and continue freezing. Check the ice every hour, scraping with a fork each time, until completely frozen. If the ice crystals are too large, leave at room temperature for 15 to 20 minutes, or until it begins to melt again, and then freeze as before.

MAKES 1 QUART

Paletas de Vainilla con Cajeta | Vanilla-Caramel Cream Pops

I heard of these *paletas* when I last visited Monterrey, but I never got to try them because for some absurd reason the ice cream shops are not open year-round. However, I thought they were an ingenious idea, so I immediately set about trying to create them. The paletas I heard about but never got to try had the caramel in the center—but recreating that effect was way too sticky and complicated to do at home. So I devised this simpler way to layer these two delicious flavors.

Combine 1½ cups of the heavy cream, the milk, sugar, scraped vanilla bean and pod (if you're using the extract don't add it now), and salt in a pot and bring to a boil over medium heat.

Whisk the egg yolks in a large heatproof bowl. Slowly whisk about half of the hot milk mixture into the yolks and stir rapidly. Return the mixture to the pot and cook over low heat, stirring continuously with a wooden spoon or heatproof spatula, until it is thickened and coats the back of a spoon, 10 to 15 minutes.

Strain through a fine-mesh sieve and stir in the remaining 1 cup heavy cream and the vanilla extract, if using. Chill over an ice bath, stirring, until cool. Place a piece of plastic wrap directly on top, refrigerate until completely cool, about 4 hours.

Warm the *cajeta* slightly so it's pourable. If you are using store-bought *cajeta* in a glass jar, unscrew the lid, screw it on again lightly, place in a pot, and fill the pot three-fourths of the way up the sides with hot water. Warm over medium-low heat and let simmer for about 5 minutes, then carefully remove the jar from the hot water with a towel. This will allow you to pour the *cajeta* much more easily.

Add a little of the custard to the ice pop molds (about a quarter of the way up), then freeze for 1 hour. Next pour in a little *cajeta*. Continue alternating the vanilla custard with the *cajeta* until the molds are filled. Use a large skewer to swirl the mixture gently. Freeze for about 3 hours, until the creamsicles begin to set. Insert the sticks and let freeze for another 4 hours at least. Unmold as directed.

MAKES 8 TO 10

2½ cups heavy cream

1½ cups whole milk

1½ cups sugar

1 vanilla bean, split lengthwise and scraped, or 2 teaspoons pure vanilla extract

Pinch of salt

7 egg yolks

¾ to 1 cup *cajeta*, homemade (page 151) or store-bought

3 ears fresh corn, shucked

2½ cups whole milk

1½ cups heavy cream

¾ cup sugar

8 egg yolks

Pinch of salt

½ teaspoon pure vanilla extract

The culinary diversity of corn is manifested in its incredible array of preparations. It's most often associated with and used in savory dishes, but it has snuck into various sweet ones, and corn ice cream is absolutely one of the best.

Be sure to take advantage of the height of corn season, because fresh corn's sweetness will seep into the flavor of the ice cream. Traditionally, this ice cream is not made with a custard base, but I believe that it enhances the creaminess of the corn.

Slice the kernels from the corn into a bowl. Break the cobs into 3 pieces and put them with the kernels into a saucepan. Add the milk, heavy cream, and ½ cup of the sugar and stir to combine. Bring to a boil over medium heat, stirring. Remove from the heat and allow to steep, covered, for 1 hour.

Remove the cobs and discard. Remove about 1 cup of the corn kernels and reserve. Purée the mixture in the pot with an immersion blender and bring to a boil over medium heat.

In a large bowl, whisk the egg yolks with the remaining ¼ cup sugar and the salt. Slowly whisk about half of the hot milk mixture into the yolk mixture and stir rapidly. Return the mixture to the pot and cook over low heat, stirring continuously with a wooden spoon or heatproof spatula, until it is thickened and coats the back of a spoon, 10 to 15 minutes. Strain through a fine-mesh sieve and press down with a wooden spoon to extract as much liquid as possible. Add the vanilla and the reserved corn kernels and stir to combine. Pour into a container, place a piece of plastic wrap directly on top, and chill over an ice bath until cool. Refrigerate, covered, until completely cool, about 3 hours, and freeze in an ice cream maker according to the manufacturer's instructions.

MAKES ABOUT 5 CUPS

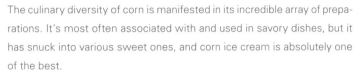

Helado de Aguacate | Avocado Ice Cream

Avocado is one of the many ingredients indigenous to the Americas, and luckily it is available in supermarkets all over the world. The Hass avocado is the creamiest and sweetest variety, but when it comes to sweet preparations, many may wonder—avocado ice cream? Most people have had avocado in a salty and/or spicy format, or at least as an accompaniment to something that is not primarily sweet. If you like avocado, however, you will really enjoy this ice cream. Its natural oil gives the ice cream a very smooth and silky mouthfeel, and the lime juice heightens its flavor. Although it may taste too sweet before freezing in the ice cream maker, it will be just right when it's done.

Peel and pit the avocados. Place the avocado flesh in a blender with the lime juice, salt, milk, and sugar. Blend until smooth. Freeze immediately in an ice cream maker according to the manufacturer's instructions.

MAKES ABOUT 1 QUART

3 ripe Hass avocados

Juice of 2 limes

Pinch of salt

1½ cups whole milk

1 cup plus 2 tablespoons sugar

2 cups goat's milk

⅓ cup sugar

1 cup heavy cream

Pinch of salt

7 egg yolks

2 teaspoons pure vanilla extract

10 ounces *cajeta*, homemade (page 151) or store-bought

¾ cup coarsely chopped toasted pecans or hazelnuts, 1 cup broken pieces *galletas maria* (found in many Latin markets) or graham crackers, or ¾ cup chopped dark chocolate (optional)

I've never met anyone who didn't like this ice cream. How could you not? This soft, creamy ice cream is so rich it makes you feel like royalty. I love the acidity of the goat's milk, but feel free to substitute cow's milk if you prefer.

Combine the milk and sugar, ½ cup of the heavy cream, and the salt in a pot and bring to a boil over medium heat. Whisk the egg yolks in a large heatproof bowl, slowly pour about half of the hot milk mixture into the yolks, whisking continuously, and then return the mixture to the pot. Cook over medium heat, stirring continuously with a wooden spoon or heatproof spatula, until it is thickened and coats the back of a spoon or spatula, 10 to 15 minutes. Stir in the vanilla extract.

Place the *cajeta* in a bowl. If you are using store-bought *cajeta* in a glass jar, unscrew the lid, screw it on again lightly, place in a pot, and fill the pot three-fourths of the way up the sides with hot water. Warm over medium-low heat and let simmer for about 5 minutes, then carefully remove the jar from the hot water with a towel. This will allow you to pour the *cajeta* much more easily.

Strain the milk mixture into the *cajeta*. Add the remaining ½ cup heavy cream, stir to combine, and chill over an ice bath, stirring continuously. Refrigerate, covered, until completely cool, about 3 hours. Freeze in an ice cream maker according to the manufacturer's instructions. Incorporate any nuts, cookies, or chocolate by hand once the ice cream has finished churning and freeze until fully set.

MAKES ABOUT 5 CUPS

Helado de Pasitas con Tequila | Tequila-Raisin Ice Cream

I did a lot of experimenting when I worked at Rosa Mexicano as the pastry chef, and trying out new ice cream flavors was one of my favorite things during my time there. I have always loved rum-raisin ice cream and thought raisins and tequila might also go well together. The *reposado* and *añejo* styles of tequila have been aged and come through very nicely, but I felt the ice cream needed another layer of flavor, so I added *canela*, which turned out to be just what was missing.

¾ cup dark raisins

¾ cup tequila (preferably *reposado* or *añejo*)

1 cup whole milk

1 (3-inch) piece *canela*

¾ cup sugar

1¾ cups heavy cream

Pinch of salt

6 egg yolks

Combine the raisins and tequila in a small saucepan and simmer over low heat for 3 minutes. Remove from the heat and let steep for at least 2 hours (this can be done the night before).

Combine the milk, *canela*, sugar, ¾ cup of the heavy cream, and the salt in a pot and bring to a boil over medium heat. Whisk the egg yolks in a large heatproof bowl. Slowly whisk about half of the hot milk mixture into the yolks and stir rapidly. Return the mixture to the pot and cook over medium heat, stirring continuously with a wooden spoon or heatproof spatula, until it is thickened and coats the back of the spoon or spatula, 10 to 15 minutes.

Strain through a fine-mesh sieve, add the remaining 1 cup heavy cream and the liquid from the macerated raisins, and stir to combine. Chill over an ice bath, stirring, until cool. Refrigerate, covered, until completely cool, about 3 hours, and freeze in an ice cream maker according to the manufacturer's instructions. Add the plumped raisins once the ice cream has finished churning and freeze until fully set.

MAKES ABOUT 1 QUART

Helado de Queso | Requesón Cheese Ice Cream

1½ cups whole milk

¼ teaspoon pure vanilla extract

⅔ cup sugar

¼ teaspoon salt

6 egg yolks

8 ounces *requesón*, *queso fresco*, or pot cheese, crumbled

The light granular texture of this tasty ice cream is what makes me love it so much. Swirl in some *cajeta* toward the end of the churning or top it with some berries if you want to add a complementary flavor, though I think it is perfect just as it is.

Combine the milk, vanilla, sugar, and salt in a small pot and bring to a boil over medium heat.

Whisk the egg yolks in a large heatproof bowl. Slowly whisk about half of the hot milk mixture into the yolks and stir rapidly. Return the mixture to the pot and cook over low heat, stirring continuously with a wooden spoon or heatproof spatula, until it is thickened and coats the back of a spoon, 10 to 15 minutes. Add the cheese and stir with a whisk until blended (you can use a hand or standing blender if you want it a little less grainy).

Chill over an ice bath, stirring, until cool. Refrigerate, covered, until completely cool, about 3 hours, and freeze in an ice cream maker according to the manufacturer's instructions.

MAKES ABOUT 3 CUPS

Sorbete de Rosas | Rose Petal Sherbet

4 ounces rose petals

3 cups whole milk or almond milk

1 cup heavy cream

1 cup sugar

The city of Oaxaca has some of the best frozen treats in Mexico, despite the fact it isn't located right near the coast. This particular recipe is adapted from one given to me by Dinorah Allende, a beautiful woman who owns Chagüita, a delicious *nevería* that has been around for five generations. Be sure to buy culinary-grade rose petals from a trusted source that doesn't use any pesticides or chemicals (the smaller petals have the most intense flavor), and get the highest-quality milk possible.

Wash the rose petals and pat dry. Reserve about one-fourth of the rose petals and blend the rest with the milk, heavy cream, and sugar. Strain through a fine-mesh sieve. Freeze in an ice cream maker according to the manufacturer's instructions. Thinly slice the reserved petals and stir into the sherbet once it has finished churning and freeze until fully set.

MAKES ABOUT 1 QUART

MEXICO MODERNO

MODERN MEXICO

HISTORY IS MADE UP OF a series of encounters with people and places. It is shaped through circumstance and time. The Mexico of today has a strong cultural heritage that was enriched by Spanish customs and ingredients.

A big transition to modernity occurred from the 1930s to the 1960s, when petroleum, gas, and electricity transformed our way of life. President Ávila Camacho forbade the use of coal for fuel, and electric stoves, aluminum pots, Pyrex, and pressure cookers soon filled Mexican kitchens. However, *comals*, *cazuelas*, *metates*, and *molcajetes* continue to be used today and are an important part of our culinary heritage.

Likewise, many of our sweet treats have been preserved through artisans who take deep pride in the land and retain an incredibly strong sense of tradition. These preparations have remained intact in many kitchens, where people continue to make the recipes that their grand-mothers, great-grandmothers, and generations before them made, and it is apparent in cook-books that are stained and sticky from use. These are the footprints of our historical and geographical past, keeping the old voices of our ancestors alive. When it comes to food, for Mexico, nostalgia always sweetens the palate.

From our present-day cultural blend has emerged a new Mexico, a Mexico that explores boundaries and gives birth to new expressions. New creations are inspired by techniques adopted and imported from other cultures, but the love for our traditional flavors remains. The addition of spicy and sour notes has transformed recipes that have remained intact since colonial times. Contemporary chefs re-create the flavors we grew up with in a whole new and unexpected way, still preserving their essence. This is not to say that our cuisine isn't rich enough as it is, but culi-nary refinement is perhaps an inevitable part of globalization.

This chapter is dedicated to this phenomenon. The recipes I created for this chapter embrace the refined techniques of other cuisines, while keeping the flavors truthful to Mexico. This evo-lution in many ways has brought us closer to each other and to our roots . . . well, at least that's the way it has been for me.

Mixiote de Pera con Hojaldre de Queso | Piloncillo-Roasted Pears with Cheese Pastry

Cheese Pastry

1 pound *requesón*, pot cheese, or fresh ricotta

¾ cup sugar

Pinch of salt

¼ cup *crema* or heavy cream

1 egg

3 ounces Manchego cheese (or any other salty hard cheese), shredded

1 recipe Quick Puff Pastry (page 164)

2 egg yolks

2 tablespoons whole milk

Roasted Pears

8 ounces *piloncillo*, chopped, or 1 cup firmly packed dark brown sugar mixed with 1 tablespoon molasses

2 cups apple or pear cider

1 (3-inch) piece *canela*

1 vanilla bean, split lengthwise

2 tablespoons unsalted butter

Pinch of salt

6 Bosc or Anjou pears (ripe but a bit on the firm side)

Banana leaves or parchment paper

My dear friend Roberto Santibañez and I have had a lot of fun over the years since we began working together at Rosa Mexicano, cooking together and creating dishes inspired by our land that we so often miss living in New York. This is one of the desserts that we still talk about.

The name for this dish comes from *mixiote,* which is the thin film from the maguey leaf that was traditionally used to wrap savory dishes that are baked or steamed, releasing the leaf's wonderful herbal sweetness. Nowadays, most *mixiotes* actually use parchment paper or banana leaves, alluding to the way the dish is prepared rather than the original definition. In this version, the pears are cooked slowly in a sweet *piloncillo* syrup inside these little pouches, and are then served warm over a slightly salty cheese filling. When the pouch is cut open, it releases the amazing syrup fragrance that balances perfectly with the flaky, buttery cheese pastry.

TO MAKE THE CHEESE PASTRY, drain the *requesón* in a cheesecloth-lined bowl. Combine the drained cheese, ¼ cup of the sugar, the salt, *crema*, and egg in a bowl and blend with a spoon or whisk. Stir in the Manchego cheese (this mixture can be made 2 days ahead of time and kept in the refrigerator).

Line 2 baking sheets with parchment paper. Roll out the puff pastry on a lightly floured surface into a rectangle about ¼ inch thick. Using a cookie cutter or large glass, cut out twelve 5-inch-diameter circles and place on the prepared baking sheets. Gather the scraps together by placing them on top of each other, overlapping a bit to stick them together (don't form into a ball!). Roll lightly into a rectangle about ¼ inch thick and cut out 4 more circles.

Preheat the oven to 375°F.

Put about 2 tablespoons of the cheese filling in the center of 8 of the circles, leaving some room around the edges. Lightly whisk the egg yolks with a fork and lightly brush the edges of the circles. Place the other circles on top and press tightly along the edges to seal. Refrigerate for 10 to 15 minutes, until firm. Lightly whisk the milk into the rest of the yolks and brush the tops of the pastries. Sprinkle with the remaining ½ cup sugar and bake until the tops and bottoms are golden, 20 to 30 minutes. Remove from the oven and transfer to a wire rack to cool. (The cheese pastries can be made and refrigerated up to 3 days in advance.) Leave the oven on at the same temperature for the pears.

CONTINUED

TO MAKE THE ROASTED PEARS, combine the *piloncillo*, cider, and *canela* in a medium-large pot. Scrape the vanilla bean with the tip of a knife and add it with the pod to the pot. Cook over medium heat, stirring, until dissolved. Whisk in the butter and salt, remove from the heat, and let cool slightly. Discard the *canela* and the vanilla pod. Peel, core, and cut the pears into ½-inch wedges and add to the mixture.

Cut the banana leaves or parchment paper into eight 6-inch squares, put about ½ cup of the pear mixture in the center of each one, bring the edges together, and twist the top. Tear a thin strip of banana leaf and use it to tie the top closed (if you're using parchment, tie the top with butcher's twine). Place the packets on a baking sheet and bake for 35 minutes. Remove from the oven and let cool for 10 minutes.

Place one packet of pears on top of each cheese pastry and cut the packet with scissors at the table so the pastry doesn't get soggy and the wonderful aroma is released. Plus, you'll have that wow factor that will impress all.

SERVES 8

Ante de Maracuya y Mezcal | Passion Fruit–Mezcal Trifle

I absolutely love passion fruit, and the trees in southeastern Mexico, particularly one in my childhood friend Fernando's backyard in Bacalar Quintana Roo, inspired this creation.

Think of this dessert like a tropical layered cake filled with the exquisite tartness of passion fruit and topped with a silky, sugary meringue. Avoid using mezcal with a worm in the bottle because they are, for the most part, not the best quality. You will need a blowtorch to caramelize the meringue topping, or you can use a broiler or simply sprinkle with some crunchy meringue instead (page 160).

TO MAKE THE JELLY, combine the passion fruit pulp, water, and sugar in a heavy small pot over medium heat and cook, stirring, until the sugar dissolves. Adjust the heat to maintain a constant simmer, and cook until the mixture is thickened and "grabs" onto a spoon, 15 to 20 minutes. Remove from the heat, add the lemon juice, and let cool

Passion Fruit Jelly

2½ cups passion fruit pulp with seeds (about 10 passion fruits)

¼ cup water

2⅓ cups sugar

1 tablespoon freshly squeezed lemon or lime juice

1 recipe *Mamón* (page 53)

1 cup mezcal

1 recipe Italian Meringue (page 144)

completely. If the jelly feels too thick once it's cooled, stir in a little bit of hot water. (The jelly can be made up to a month in advance and stored in the refrigerator.)

To assemble the *ante*, slice the *mamón* horizontally across into 3 even layers. Brush each layer a few times with the mezcal. Place one cake layer on a serving platter, spread one-third of the passion fruit jelly on top, spreading evenly to the edges. Place another cake layer on top, spread with another third of the jelly, and repeat for the last layer. Spread the meringue over the sides and top of the cake with an offset spatula, moving the meringue around so it looks like waves or flames. Finish by toasting the meringue waves with a kitchen torch. Dip a knife into hot water before making each slice so the meringue doesn't stick to it.

SERVES 8 TO 10

Capirotada de Mango con Salsa de Tamarindo | Mango Bread Pudding with Tamarind Sauce

I used the idea of the delicious brittle caramel topping that defines a crème brûlée on this bread pudding simply because I love it! You will need a propane or butane torch to caramelize the sugar that will top the delicious layers of toasted buttery bread with fresh mango held together by a fragrant custard. The sweet and sour flavors of the sauce go wonderfully with the richness of the custard and heighten the freshness of the sweet yellow fruit.

Preheat the oven to 350°F.

TO MAKE THE BREAD PUDDING, peel the skin from the 1-pound mango using a vegetable peeler and slice off the thicker end to make a base so it can stand up. Hold the narrow tip with one hand and slice the mango into evenly thick slices (about ¼ inch) on each side (use a mandoline if you have one). Reserve the slices.

Slice off the thicker end of the ½-pound mango to make a base so it can stand up. Holding the mango firmly, slice downward with a sharp knife as close to the seed as possible; repeat on the other side. Scoop out the flesh with a large spoon and purée in a blender or food processor. Strain through a fine-mesh sieve only if you have any fibrous bits.

Dice the bread into ¼-inch cubes, lay them in a single layer on a baking sheet, and toast in the oven until dry (it's okay if they color a little). Remove from the oven and let cool.

Meanwhile, heat the brandy in a small pan over low heat until it begins to bubble around the edges. Remove from the heat, add the dried cherries and raisins, and soak until softened, about 20 minutes.

Combine the half-and-half, 1¼ cups of the sugar, *canela*, and salt in a pot and bring to a boil over medium heat. In a large heatproof bowl, whisk the eggs. Strain half of the hot mixture into the eggs, whisk briskly, then strain the remaining hot mixture into the eggs. Add the mango purée, bread cubes, macerated fruit with any remaining liquid, and the vanilla. Stir well to combine, and let sit for at least 30 minutes.

Preheat the oven to 350°F. Butter the bottom and sides of a 9-inch cake pan and dust with sugar, tapping out the excess.

Lay the mango slices all around the bottom of the pan, overlapping so there are no holes. Spoon the bread pudding mixture on top and press gently so the top is even and the mixture reaches the bottom.

Put the cake pan in a larger baking dish and carefully pour hot water to fill up three-fourths of the way up the sides (I like to do this right in

Bread Pudding

1 (1-pound) mango and
1 (½-pound) mango
(ripe but a bit firm)

1 brioche or challah bread

½ cup brandy, dark rum,
or tequila

⅓ cup dried cherries

⅓ cup black raisins

4 cups half-and-half

1¼ cups plus 2 tablespoons sugar

1 (3-inch) piece *canela*

Pinch of salt

9 eggs

½ teaspoon pure vanilla extract

Tamarind Sauce

½ cup tamarind pulp with seeds

1½ cups water

½ cup honey

3 tablespoons dark brown sugar

Pinch of salt

the oven so I don't spill it). Bake until firm to the touch and a toothpick inserted into the center comes out clean, about 40 minutes.

Remove the pan from the water and allow to cool completely before unmolding. Run a sharp knife around the edges, place a serving plate or dish over the pan, and rapidly but carefully flip over. Refrigerate the bread pudding for at least 1 hour before caramelizing the top of it. (You can make the bread pudding up to this point and refrigerate overnight, covered.)

Sprinkle the 2 tablespoons sugar on top of the mango slices, creating an even layer. Holding a blowtorch about 2 inches from the top, melt the sugar, moving the blowtorch evenly across the surface until the sugar is golden and caramelized. Allow to cool slightly, 1 to 2 minutes, and lightly score the slices you want. Basically, you want to cut through the sugar before it hardens so it doesn't crack. If the sugar sticks to the knife, wait a little longer and try again. Wipe off the knife between slices, if necessary.

TO MAKE THE TAMARIND SAUCE, combine the tamarind pulp and water in a small-medium saucepan and bring to a boil over medium heat, stirring. Pass the mixture through a strainer, pressing to remove the seeds and all the fibers. Stir in the honey, brown sugar, and salt. Let cool. Add a bit more hot water if it is too thick (it should be thick but pourable).

Serve each slice with sauce alongside.

SERVES 10 TO 12

Tres Leches de Ron con Chocolate | Chocolate Rum Tres Leches Cake

This is another cake that I developed when I worked at Rosa Mexicano, and it quickly became one of the most popular desserts. We used to serve it with caramelized bananas, whipped cream, and chocolate sauce, all on the side. I have since tweaked the recipe a bit, by adding some chocolate to the *tres leches* mixture itself, instead of having a separate sauce, and by layering the cake with whipped cream.

Preheat the oven to 325°F.

TO MAKE THE CAKE, bring the water to a boil and stir in the instant coffee, mixing until it dissolves. Put the cocoa in a heatproof bowl and pour the hot coffee into it, whisking until there are no lumps; set aside to cool.

In a large bowl, sift together the flour, baking powder, baking soda, salt, and half of the sugar. In a separate bowl, combine the egg yolks, oil, and vanilla. Add the cooled cocoa mixture and gently stir with a whisk until smooth. Pour the egg mixture into the large bowl with the flour mixture, whisking until the batter is smooth. In a separate bowl, beat the egg whites with the salt and the cream of tartar until it starts to thicken. Add the remaining half of the sugar gradually and continue beating until stiff and glossy peaks form.

Stir about one-third of the egg whites into the batter to lighten the mixture, then add the remaining egg whites in two parts, folding gently but making sure everything is well incorporated. Divide the batter into 2 ungreased 9-inch pans and bake until a toothpick inserted into the center comes out clean, 50 to 60 minutes. As soon as they come out of the oven, unmold the cakes onto a wire rack, and let them sit until cool. Remove the pans and prepare the *tres leches* mixture.

TO MAKE THE TRES LECHES, bring the half-and-half to a boil in a small saucepan over medium heat. Put the chopped chocolate in a heatproof bowl and pour the hot half-and-half over. Allow to sit for a minute, then stir with a whisk until smooth. Whisk in the evaporated milk, salt, condensed milk, and rum, blending well. Put the cakes in a deep dish or back into their baking pans and pour the warm mixture over them. Be sure to pour any liquid that dripped down the sides on top of the cakes as well. Cover with plastic wrap and refrigerate for 2 to 4 hours, or freeze for 30 to 40 minutes, so they are easier to handle.

TO MAKE THE FILLING, beat the heavy cream with an electric mixer or by hand until slightly thickened. Add the confectioner's

Cake

¾ cup water

2 teaspoons instant coffee crystals

½ cup unsweetened cocoa powder, preferably Dutch processed

1¾ cups cake flour

2 teaspoons baking powder

½ teaspoon baking soda

½ teaspoon salt

1¼ cups sugar

5 egg yolks

½ cup vegetable oil

1 teaspoon pure vanilla extract

8 egg whites

Pinch of salt

¾ teaspoon cream of tartar

Tres Leches

1 cup half-and-half

4 ounces semisweet chocolate, finely chopped

1 (12-ounce) can evaporated milk

Pinch of salt

1 (14-ounce) can sweetened condensed milk

½ cup dark rum

Filling

1⅓ cups heavy cream

¼ cup confectioner's sugar

½ teaspoon pure vanilla extract,
or ½ vanilla bean, scraped

1 (2- to 4-ounce) piece semisweet
chocolate, for shaving

sugar and vanilla and continue beating until thickened and smooth. Refrigerate until the cakes have cooled.

To assemble the cake, put one of the cakes on a piece of cardboard or a serving platter and spread about one-third of the filling evenly on top. Top with the second cake and cover the top and sides with the remaining filling. Holding the chocolate with a paper towel in one hand, use a peeler to shave the chocolate onto the cake.

SERVES 10 TO 12

Pastel Volteado de Plátano Macho | Upside-Down Plantain Cake

3½ cups sugar

⅓ cup water

2 ripe but firm plantains
(see note, page 196)

2 cups all-purpose flour

2½ tablespoons baking powder

½ teaspoon freshly
ground _canela_

¼ teaspoon salt

¼ cup unsalted butter,
at room temperature

2 eggs

2 teaspoons pure vanilla extract

1 cup whole milk

I love plantains! I love them fried, steamed, and even raw (although if I eat too many this way, I get a stomach ache). Whenever I see some black ripe ones, I buy many and figure I'll eat them one way or another. I went crazy one day last year in Mexico and ate them every way I could think of. Then I had my aha moment! I thought that whatever desserts are tasty with bananas must also be good with plantains, so I played around a bit and decided that the upside-down cake was the best way to go. I think it's great on its own, but you can serve it with a little _crema_ as well.

Preheat the oven to 350°F. Combine 2 cups of the sugar and the water in a small, heavy saucepan. Cover and bring to a boil over medium-low heat, then remove the lid to release the steam, which will help avoid crystallization. Continue cooking until the sugar dissolves and turns a dark golden color, then swirl the mixture around so it caramelizes evenly. Pour into an 8-inch cake pan and allow it to set for a few minutes. Meanwhile, peel and cut the plantains into slightly diagonal slices about ¼ inch thick. Arrange them over the caramel, in slightly overlapping concentric circles, covering the bottom. (If you have any leftover plantain, mash it and set it aside.)

Sift together the flour, baking powder, _canela_, and salt into a bowl and whisk to incorporate. In a separate bowl with a mixer, or in a standing mixer, cream together the butter and the remaining 1½ cups sugar until light and fluffy. Add the eggs one at a time, then add the vanilla and any mashed plantain (don't add more than ⅓ cup), blending until well incorporated. Add about one-third of the flour mixture,

CONTINUED

alternating with one-third of the milk, and blend to combine, adding the remaining flour mixture and milk in two more batches. Pour the batter over the plantains and bake until a toothpick inserted into the center comes out clean and the cake bounces back when pressed lightly in the center, 50 to 60 minutes.

Let cool for 5 to 10 minutes, run a small knife around the edges, put a serving plate on top, and carefully flip over. Serve warm or at room temperature.

SERVES 8 TO 10

> When plantains are ripe they turn black (but make sure they aren't moldy) and this means they are at their sweetest state. Be sure to pick some that have a black peel but can still hold their shape when you cut them.

Terrina Helada Roja con Jamaica |
Red Sorbet Terrine with Hibiscus Compote

"Terrine" is the name given to a specific mold commonly used in French cuisine, but its definition has changed over time. I like to play around and use different molds shaped like triangles, ovals, and rectangles.

I love the vibrant color of the hibiscus flower and I think its tart flavor complements many other fruits. I chose these particular flavors because they go quite nicely together and because I've always thought different shades of one color suggest a subtle elegance.

TO MAKE THE PINK GRAPEFRUIT SORBET, combine the water and sugar in a small pot and cook over medium heat, stirring, until the sugar has dissolved. Remove from the heat and let cool slightly. Whisk in the juice and refrigerate until completely cool. Freeze in an ice cream maker according to the manufacturer's instructions. Divide the frozen sorbet in half and freeze in separate containers.

TO MAKE THE RASPBERRY SORBET, combine the water and sugar in a small pot and cook over medium heat, stirring, until the sugar has dissolved. Remove from the heat and let cool slightly. Purée the raspberries with the lime juice in a blender, strain through a fine-mesh sieve, pressing to extract as much juice as possible, and discard the seeds. Whisk in the cooled syrup and refrigerate until completely cool. Freeze in an ice cream maker according to the manufacturer's instructions. Divide the frozen sorbet in half and freeze in separate containers.

TO MAKE THE HIBISCUS COMPOTE, combine the hibiscus flowers, water, sugar, and vanilla bean (scrape with the tip of a knife

Pink Grapefruit Sorbet

½ cup water

1¼ cups sugar

3 cups pink grapefruit juice (preferably freshly squeezed)

Raspberry Sorbet

1 cup water

¾ cup sugar

3 cups fresh raspberries

1 tablespoon freshly squeezed lime or lemon juice

Hibiscus Compote

1½ cups hibiscus flowers

6 cups water

¾ cup sugar

1 vanilla bean, split lengthwise

1 tablespoon unflavored gelatin

Candied Hibiscus

1 cup reserved flowers
from compote

½ cup water

1½ cups sugar

2 to 3 cups sliced or chopped
mixed berries

and add it with the pod) in a pot. Bring to a boil over medium heat and cook until reduced to 4 cups, 20 to 25 minutes. Remove from the heat and let steep for 30 minutes. Remove the vanilla bean and reserve for another use. Sprinkle the gelatin over the water and let stand for a couple of minutes to soften. Stir to combine, strain, reserve 1 cup of the flowers, and let cool completely (add a bit more water to make 4 cups if you've reduced it too much).

TO MAKE THE CANDIED HIBISCUS, lay the reserved hibiscus flowers on a rack to dry for 1 hour. Combine the water and 1 cup of the sugar in a small pot and cook over medium heat, stirring, until the sugar has dissolved and the syrup has thickened, about 5 minutes. Remove from the heat and let cool slightly. Add the hibiscus flowers, stir to combine, and lay on a rack to dry for 1 hour. Toss with the remaining ½ cup sugar and allow to set. (This can be made ahead of time and stored in an airtight container in a dry area for up to 3 days.)

To assemble the terrine, lightly oil a 12 by 4½ by 3-inch loaf pan and line the bottom and sides with plastic wrap (use 2 or 3 pieces, if necessary), leaving about 3 inches overhanging all around. Freeze for 15 minutes.

Thaw one of the grapefruit sorbet containers in the refrigerator until you can spread it but it is still frozen, about 30 minutes. Scoop it into the prepared pan and spread in an even layer using an offset spatula. Freeze until firm. Meanwhile, thaw one of the raspberry sorbet containers in the refrigerator in the same manner. Spread in an even layer, freeze until firm, and repeat the process once more, alternating flavors. When the last layer of sorbet is spread, cover the whole thing with the plastic wrap that was overhanging and freeze overnight (this can be made up to 1 week in advance).

When ready to serve, unwrap the top and invert the pan onto a chilled serving dish. Allow to sit for a few minutes so it thaws out enough for you to remove the pan (you could also dampen a cloth with hot water, wring it out, and place it all around for a minute or so). Peel off the plastic wrap and slice into the desired thickness (you can slice these ahead of time, placing a piece of parchment paper between each slice and storing in an airtight container in the freezer).

To serve, put some of the mixed berries on a plate, lean or rest a slice of terrine on top, and scatter with a couple of candied flowers. Pass the compote at the table.

SERVES 10 TO 12

Almond Cakes

½ cup almond flour

1½ cups granulated sugar

1⅓ cups cake flour

1 teaspoon baking powder

½ cup water

½ cup plus 3 tablespoons
vegetable oil

4 egg yolks

7 egg whites

Chocolate Cake

⅔ cup cake flour

½ cup unsweetened
cocoa powder, preferably
Dutch processed

6 eggs

1 cup granulated sugar

½ cup unsalted butter, melted

1 teaspoon pure vanilla extract

Crunchy Layer

3 cups hazelnut-chocolate spread
like Nutella (you'll need the
large 26.5-ounce jar)

3 cups plain crispy rice cereal

Ganache

1½ cups heavy cream

12 ounces semisweet
chocolate, finely chopped

2 tablespoons tequila
(preferably *reposado* or *añejo*)

I developed this recipe several years ago. My training was mostly French, and I wanted to take one of the classic French desserts and give it a Mexican flavor. The different layers of textures and flavors come together beautifully and show off the cake's sophistication when it is cut into beautiful rectangles. It takes quite a bit of time to make because there are many steps, but it can all be prepared in advance and will come together very nicely. It is well worth the effort. Note that you will need 4 baking sheets of the same size.

TO MAKE THE ALMOND CAKES, preheat the oven to 400°F. Lightly grease 2 baking sheets and line with parchment paper. Heavily butter the paper and dust with flour, tapping out the excess.

Whisk together the almond flour, ½ cup of the granulated sugar, the cake flour, and the baking powder in a bowl. In a separate bowl, combine the water, oil, and egg yolks. Beat the egg whites with a mixer on high speed until starting to thicken but not yet forming soft peaks, gradually add the remaining 1 cup sugar, and continue to beat until medium peaks form.

Add the flour mixture to the yolk mixture and blend well. Fold in the egg whites. Spread on the prepared baking sheets as evenly as possible with an offset spatula and bake until they spring back to the touch, 8 to 12 minutes. Let cool.

Loosen the edges of one of the cakes with a paring knife. Place a piece of parchment or wax paper on top and carefully but rapidly flip over. Peel the parchment paper away carefully and flip over again. Repeat with the second cake.

TO MAKE THE CHOCOLATE CAKE, preheat the oven to 350°F. Lightly grease a baking sheet and line with parchment paper. Heavily butter the paper and dust with flour, tapping out the excess.

Whisk together the flour and cocoa powder in a bowl and then sift. Combine the eggs and granulated sugar in a metal bowl and set over a pot of simmering water (the water shouldn't touch the bowl); whisk until warm to the touch, 3 to 5 minutes. Remove from the heat and continue beating (a stand mixer works best for this) until tripled in volume and a ribbon forms when you lift the beaters, 5 to 8 minutes. In a separate bowl, combine the melted butter and vanilla and keep warm.

Place the bowl with the egg mixture on a kitchen towel to prevent it from sliding and add the cocoa mixture in thirds, alternating with the

CONTINUED

butter mixture, folding with a whisk or spatula until just combined. Spread on the prepared baking sheet as evenly as possible with an offset spatula and bake until it springs back to the touch, 5 to 7 minutes. Let cool.

Loosen the edges of the cake with a paring knife. Place a piece of parchment or wax paper on top and carefully but rapidly flip over. Peel the parchment paper away carefully and flip over again. If you are making the *opereta* ahead of time, put each layer of cake between two pieces of parchment paper. You can stack them on top of one another, but keep the layers on a tray so they are flat. Wrap well in plastic wrap.

TO MAKE THE CRUNCHY LAYER, open the Nutella jar, remove the aluminum cover, and close it again but not too tightly. Fill a small pot halfway with water and bring to a simmer over low heat. Place the jar in the water and heat until melted. Pour the Nutella into a measuring cup to reach 3 cups. Put the Nutella in a bowl, add the rice cereal, and stir until well combined. Lightly grease the back of a baking sheet and line with parchment paper. Pour the Nutella-covered cereal in the center, put another piece of parchment paper on top, and spread evenly to all edges with a rolling pin (enjoy any excess that may peek over the edges). Freeze until set, 30 to 40 minutes.

TO MAKE THE GANACHE, scald the heavy cream in a saucepan over medium heat. Place the chocolate in a heatproof bowl and pour the heavy cream over; let stand for 3 minutes. Whisk until smooth, then add the tequila. (If making ahead, let it come to room temperature or reheat it slightly in the microwave until it is a spreadable consistency.)

TO MAKE THE BUTTERCREAM, combine the butter and confectioner's sugar in the bowl of a stand mixer with the whisk attachment. Beat on medium-low speed until blended. Increase the speed to medium and continue to beat, scraping the sides as necessary, for 3 minutes. Add the *canela* and 2 tablespoons of the heavy cream and whip for 1 to 2 minutes longer. Add the remaining 1 tablespoon heavy cream, if needed, to make a spreadable consistency. (If making ahead, let it come to room temperature or reheat it slightly in the microwave until it is a spreadable consistency.)

TO MAKE THE TEQUILA SYRUP, combine the tequila and granulated sugar in a small saucepan and cook over low heat, stirring, until the sugar has dissolved, being careful so that the tequila doesn't catch fire (if it does, simply cover it immediately with a lid). (If making ahead, reheat it on the stove or in a microwave before using.)

Buttercream

¾ cup unsalted butter (6 ounces), cut into pieces

3 cups confectioner's sugar, sifted

1 teaspoon freshly ground *canela*

2 to 3 tablespoons heavy cream

Tequila Syrup

2 cups tequila (preferably *reposado* or *añejo*)

½ cup granulated sugar

To assemble the cake, turn a baking sheet upside down or use a cutting board as a cake stand. Pour one-third of the warm tequila syrup over one of the almond cakes and let it soak in. Spread with half of the warm ganache and allow to cool slightly (you can refrigerate it if you want to speed the process). Place another almond cake on top and moisten with another third of the syrup. Let it soak in, and then spread with half of the buttercream.

Take the crunchy layer out of the freezer and carefully peel away the paper. Flip it onto the cake and carefully peel away the remaining paper. If you have a blowtorch, lightly warm the crunchy layer so the cake adheres to it (otherwise, you can rub your hands on top or be patient and wait). When the crunchy layer has softened, place the chocolate cake on top and moisten with the remaining one-third syrup.

Place a sheet of parchment or wax paper on top of the cake, place 2 full baking sheets on top, and weight with a couple of cutting boards (you want to press the layers together slightly, but not use too much weight or the cake will collapse). Refrigerate for at least 1 hour.

Remove from the refrigerator; remove the weights, pans, and parchment paper, place a baking sheet upside down on top; and carefully but rapidly flip over. Spread with the remaining half of the buttercream and freeze until set, 10 to 15 minutes.

Warm the remaining half of the ganache in a water bath or the microwave and spread on top rapidly because it will harden.

Using a ruler, measure as many ½ by 3½-inch pieces as you can (you should have around 30 when you cut the edges so that all pieces are straight). Cut, dipping a sharp knife into very hot water and quickly drying with a towel between each slice (this will make nice clean edges).

SERVES 30

Tarta de Limón con Cerezas Borrachas | Lime Tart with Drunken Cherries

It's no surprise that lime is used widely in Mexican cooking, although it can be confusing because the translation is *limón*. We don't have the yellow lemon (well, it is very rare). Lime's lovely puckery, tart flavor is celebrated in many of our preparations, including this one.

The filling for the tart is essentially a curd with a creamy texture and a bright flavor. I don't like to hide the qualities of the lime at all, and I love the combination of cherries with it. I originally made the fruit mixture with *capulines*, dark-fleshed wild cherries with large pits, but I've never seen them outside Mexico; regular cherries or blueberries are a tasty substitute.

Roll out the dough on a lightly floured surface, with a lightly floured rolling pin, until it's about 12 inches round and ¼ inch thick. Place in a 9-inch tart mold, pressing the dough to the edges. Trim the edges with a small sharp knife and refrigerate for 30 minutes.

While the crust chills, preheat the oven to 375°F.

Prick the dough lightly with a fork. Line the chilled shell with a piece of parchment paper or aluminum foil, leaving 1-inch overhang on all sides. Fill it with pie weights, dried beans, or rice (this will prevent it from bubbling). Bake until the edges are pale golden, about 20 minutes. Carefully remove the parchment with the weights and continue baking until deep golden all around, about 12 minutes longer. Remove from the oven and let cool.

TO MAKE THE FILLING, put about 2 inches of water in a medium-size saucepan and bring to a boil. In a large heatproof bowl, whisk together the eggs, egg yolks, sugar, salt, and lime juice. Set the bowl over the saucepan (it shouldn't touch the water) and whisk continuously (hold the bowl with one hand and the whisk with the other) until the mixture has thickened (turn the bowl often so there's even heat) and you can see a trail left by the whisk in the bottom of the bowl. Remove from the heat and whisk in the butter a little at a time until the mixture is smooth. Strain through a fine-mesh sieve if there are any lumps and pour directly into the cooled tart shell.

Turn on the broiler and place the tart on the top shelf of the oven; leave the oven door slightly ajar. Turn the tart carefully as it starts to brown (this won't take long at all, so be very careful), and then remove from the oven. Allow to cool for at least 1 hour.

1 recipe empanada dough (page 133)

Filling

3 eggs, cold

3 egg yolks, cold

¾ cup sugar

¼ teaspoon salt

½ cup freshly squeezed lime juice

7 tablespoons cold unsalted butter, cut into pieces

Drunken Cherries

3 cups pitted cherries or blueberries

⅓ cup confectioner's sugar

1 vanilla bean

1 teaspoon grated lime zest

⅓ cup tequila (preferably *reposado* or *añejo*)

TO MAKE THE DRUNKEN CHERRIES, place the cherries in a medium-large pan. Sift the confectioner's sugar on top, place over medium heat, and stir lightly. Split the vanilla bean lengthwise, scrape the seeds into the pan with the tip of a knife, and add the pod. Cook, stirring occasionally, until the sugar dissolves and the mixture thickens slightly, about 5 minutes. Add the lime zest and turn off the heat. Remove the pod, stir in the tequila, and set aside (this can be made up to 3 days in advance). Serve at room temperature or slightly warm.

Serve at room temperature or chilled with the drunken cherries on the side.

SERVES 10 TO 12

Pastel de Queso con Membrillo Picosito | Cheesecake with Spiced Quince

Cheesecake is one of my favorite desserts, and I love the kind that is a little bit sour. This one is made with a little *crema* and a hazelnut crust. I like to serve it with quince, a natural pairing with cheese. I also gave it a little heat from arbol chiles to showcase the wonderful combination of sweet, sour, and spicy that is popular in modern Mexico.

Preheat the oven to 350°F. Lightly grease the bottom and sides of a 9 by 3-inch springform pan and cover the outside with heavy-duty foil to prevent leakage.

TO MAKE THE CRUST, combine the brown sugar, salt, flour, and hazelnuts in a food processor and pulse until the hazelnuts are coarsely ground. Add the butter and pulse until the butter is the size of a pea and looks like coarse meal. Add 1 tablespoon of the cold water, pulse again, and check to see whether the dough comes together when you press it with your fingers. If it doesn't, add the remaining 1 tablespoon cold water and pulse to combine. Press the dough in an even layer into the bottom of the prepared pan and bake until golden, 20 to 30 minutes. Let cool on a wire rack while you prepare the filling.

TO MAKE THE FILLING, place the cream cheese in the bowl of a stand mixer with the paddle attachment and beat until smooth, 2 to 3 minutes. Add the granulated sugar, vanilla, salt, *canela*, *crema*, and cornstarch, and mix until blended, 2 to 3 minutes. Add the eggs, one at a time, and mix on low speed, scraping the sides of the bowl as needed, until blended. You do not want any lumps.

Pour the filling into the prepared crust and place inside a large roasting pan. Fill with hot water about halfway up the sides. (I like to do this right in the oven to prevent any spilling; just pull out the rack a little and hold it with one hand while pouring in the water with the other.) Bake until the filling is just set, 50 to 55 minutes, and turn off the oven. Prop open the oven door with a wooden spoon and leave the cake inside for an additional hour. Remove from the water, take off the foil, and let cool on a rack. Refrigerate for at least 3 hours before serving.

TO MAKE THE SPICED QUINCE, peel, core (save the cores), and cut the quinces into slices about 1 inch thick. Put the slices in a pot with the granulated sugar and cook over medium-low heat, stirring gently, until the sugar has dissolved. Add the lemon zest, chiles, and reserved quince cores (this will give it a nice deep color) to the pot. Bring the mixture to a boil, decrease the heat to low, and continue cooking, stirring occasionally, until a thick syrup has formed, 10 to

Crust

¼ cup firmly packed light brown sugar

Pinch of salt

1 cup all-purpose flour

½ cup hazelnuts, skins removed

½ cup cold unsalted butter, cubed

1 to 2 tablespoons cold water

Filling

1½ pounds cream cheese, at room temperature

1¼ cups granulated sugar

1 teaspoon pure vanilla extract

¼ teaspoon salt

½ teaspoon freshly ground *canela*

½ cup crema

1 tablespoon cornstarch

4 eggs, at room temperature

Spiced Quince

5 quinces

3 cups granulated sugar

Zest from 1 lemon

2 dried arbol chiles

15 minutes. Remove and discard the lemon zest, chiles, and quince cores and let cool.

To unmold the cheesecake, gently run a small thin-blade knife around the edges. Remove the ring part of the mold and slice the cake, dipping the knife in hot water and wiping the blade clean before cutting each slice. Serve on a plate with a little of the candied quince on the top or side.

SERVES 10 TO 12

Boca Negra Picosito con Salsa Dulce de Tomatillo | Spiced Chocolate Cakes with Sweet Tomatillo Sauce

Cakes

6 dried chipotle chiles

10 ounces high-quality semisweet chocolate, finely chopped

6 tablespoons freshly squeezed orange juice

1 cup sugar

¾ cup unsalted butter, cut into small pieces

4 eggs

1½ tablespoons all-purpose flour

Pinch of salt

Tomatillo Sauce

1 pound small fresh tomatillos

1 vanilla bean, split lengthwise

8 ounces *piloncillo*

⅓ cup water

¼ cup sugar

1 (3-inch) piece *canela*

I wanted to include a dessert where chocolate was the main ingredient because, well, because people love it. This recipe was previously published in *Rosa's New Mexican Table* by Roberto Santibañez and is one of my proudest creations.

The tomatillo sauce may seem unusual, but trust me, you will be pleasantly surprised, and the smokiness of the chipotles gives an incredible depth to this scrumptious dessert. *Boca negra* cake got its name because, once you dig in, your mouth will be covered in luxurious chocolate. Be sure to use high-quality chocolate because it will make all the difference in the world. Serve it as is or with a bit of lightly sweetened whipped cream, vanilla ice cream, or Natilla (page 163).

Preheat the oven to 325°F. Butter the bottom and sides of eight 4-ounce ramekins or one 9-inch cake pan (not a springform pan) and dust with sugar, tapping out the excess.

TO MAKE THE CAKES, remove the stems, seeds, and veins of the chiles and toast them flat in a hot skillet over medium heat for 2 to 3 minutes until fragrant, flipping them so they don't burn. Transfer to a bowl, cover with very hot water, and let soak until softened, 20 to 30 minutes. Drain, reserve the liquid, and purée the chiles in a blender or food processor, adding a bit of the liquid as needed to form a smooth paste. Press through a fine-mesh sieve if the paste isn't completely smooth. You will only need 1½ tablespoons of the paste, but you can freeze the rest for later use.

CONTINUED

Place the chocolate in a large heatproof bowl. Combine the orange juice and sugar in a small pot over medium heat and cook, stirring, until the sugar has dissolved. Pour over the chocolate and stir until melted and combined. (I like to use a whisk, but don't beat it, simply stir.) Add the butter, little by little, and stir until melted. Whisk in the eggs, one at a time, then add 1½ tablespoons chipotle paste and the flour and salt, stirring until smooth. Pour into the prepared ramekins.

Place the ramekins, evenly spaced, in a towel-lined baking dish to prevent them from sliding. Carefully pour hot water to fill three-fourths of the way up the sides. Bake until a thin, crusty layer forms on top and the cakes are set, 40 to 45 minutes. If using a cake pan it should take 50 to 55 minutes to bake. Remove the baking dish from the oven and remove the ramekins with a towel or tongs. Let cool for 10 minutes. Meanwhile, make the sauce.

TO MAKE THE TOMATILLO SAUCE, remove the husks from the tomatillos, rinse them under cold water, dry with a towel, and coarsely chop them. Put them in a pot, scrape the vanilla bean into the pot and add the pod, and add the *piloncillo*, water, sugar, and *canela*. Cook over medium heat, stirring from time to time, until the tomatillos are very tender, 15 to 20 minutes. Remove and discard the vanilla pod and *canela*. Transfer to a food processor and purée to the desired consistency (completely smooth or a bit chunky). Let cool. (This can be made up to a week in advance and stored in the refrigerator in an airtight container. If it is too thick, add a bit of water until it is a pourable consistency.) Serve slightly warm or at room temperature.

To unmold the cakes, dip a small, sharp knife into hot water, dry it quickly, and run it around the edges. Dip the bottom of the ramekins or cake pan into very hot water for about 1 minute (a bit longer if using a cake pan) and unmold onto plates. Be careful because they are fragile and will be difficult to move once they are unmolded. Chill in the refrigerator for at least 40 minutes if using ramekins, 1 hour if using a cake pan.

To slice the cake, dip a sharp knife into very hot water and quickly dry with a towel between each slice (this will make nice clean edges). Serve the unmolded cakes at room temperature with sauce on the side.

MAKES 8 INDIVIDUAL SERVINGS OR ONE 9-INCH CAKE (SERVES 10 TO 12)

Many large chain supermarkets have an increasingly greater selection of Latin foods. There are also countless Latin stores, Mexican delis, and ethnic specialty shops where you can find many of the ingredients and equipment you will need for this book.

Here are a few places that might help you find most of the things you'll need in case you have a hard time finding them locally.

www.ams.usda.gov
Lists farmers' markets across the United States.

Chefs' Warehouse
www.chefswarehouse.com
High-end and specialty ingredients, from chocolate to oils and nuts.

A Cook's Wares
(800) 915-9788
www.cookswares.com
A mail-order catalog of kitchen supplies, including ice cream machines, standing mixers, spice/coffee grinders, and baking sheets.

Flying Pigs Farm
246 Sutherland Road
Shushan, NY 12873
(518) 854-3844
www.flyingpigsfarm.com
Pork products from heritage breeds. Great source for leaf lard.

Gourmetsleuth
P.O. Box 508
Los Gatos, CA 95031
(408) 354-8281
www.gourmetsleuth.com
A wide selection of Mexican ingredients, tips, recipes, and items such as cornhusks, *piloncillo*, and *metates*.

The House on the Hill
650 West Grand Avenue, Unit 110
Elmhurst, IL 60126
(877) 279-4455
www.houseonthehill.net
Large selection of molds, cutters, rolling pins, and specialty pastry tools.

J.B. Prince Company
36 East 31st Street
New York, NY 10016
(800) 473-0577
www.jbprince.com
Specialty equipment including sugar thermometers, special molds, copper pots, and fine-mesh strainers.

Kalustyans
123 Lexington Avenue
New York, NY, 10016
(800) 352-3451
www.kalustyans.com
Specialty store with an incredible list of items from all over the world. They sell all kinds of rice, extracts, and chiles.

King Arthur Flour
135 Route 5 South
Norwich, VT 05055-0876
(800) 827-6836
www.kingarthurflour.com
Baking ingredients, including different flours and sugars, as well as kitchen supplies such as scales, bench scrapers, and cutters.

L'Epicerie
(866) 350-7575
www.lepicerie.com
Gourmet foods, including a wide assortment of fruit purées, chestnut purée, and nuts.

Live Superfoods
63075 Crusher Avenue, Unit 101
Bend, OR 97701
(800) 481-5074
www.livesuperfoods.com
Very specialized food products considered "superfoods," including good-quality raw cacao beans, nuts, and some dried fruits.

Melissa Guerra
4100 North 2nd Street, Suite 200
McAllen, TX 78504
(877) 875-2665
www.melissaguerra.com
This retail operation has some good-quality Mexican kitchen equipment, including tamale steamers, *comales*, and ice pop molds.

Mexgrocer
4060 Morena Boulevard, Suite C
San Diego, CA 92117
(877) 463-9476
www.mexgrocer.com
Offers all kinds of Mexican equipment, cooking tips, and authentic Mexican products, including *pinole*, *chocolate de mesa*, *molinillos*, and chiles.

Nielsen-Massey Vanillas
1550 Shields Drive
Waukegan, IL 60085
(800) 525-7873
www.nielsenmassey.com
High-quality vanilla in all its presentations from all over the world and some extracts including pure Mexican vanilla and orange blossom water.

Nu-World Foods
(630) 369-6819
www.nuworldamaranth.com
Source for puffed amaranth.

Penzeys Spices
(800) 741-7787
www.penzeysspices.com
Enormous variety of spices, including Ceylon cinnamon and ground chile peppers.

The Perfect Purée of Napa Valley
2700 Napa Valley Corporate Drive, Suite L
Napa, CA 94558
(800) 556-3707
www.perfectpuree.com
Fruit-based products, mainly purées, including prickly pear, tamarind, and mango; they also carry lemon and orange zest and concentrates.

www.safeeggs.com
(800) 410-7619
Pasteurized eggs in the shell.

Taza Chocolate
561 Windsor Street
Somerville, MA 02143-4192
(617) 623-0804
www.tazachocolate.com
Organic stone ground chocolate for hot chocolate.

BIBLIOGRAPHY

Artes de Mexico, *La cocina Mexicana* II. Mexico City, Mexico: Litográfica Torres y Rosas, 1960.

Azcué y Mancera, Ing. Luis. *El chocolate.* Monograph.

Bali, Jaime and Niurka Bali. *Mexico dulzura y alegría.* Mexico City, Mexico: MVS Editorial, 2008.

Barros, Cristina and Mónica del Villar. *El santo olor de la panadería.* Mexico City, Mexico: Fernández Cueto Editores, 1992.

Bauman, Henry J. *Alcohol in Ancient Mexico.* Salt Lake City: The University of Utah Press, 2000.

Chapa, Martha. *Bebidas Mexicanas,* León, Spain: Editorial Everest, 1999.

Colmenares, Ana María Guzmán de Vásquez. *La cocina de Colima.* Mexico City, Mexico: Litógrafos Unidos, 1987.

D'Angeli, Alicia Gironella and Jorge D'Angeli,. *Gran Larousse de la cocina Mexicana,* Mexico City, Mexico: Ediciones Larousse, 1994.

de Exhague, María Mestayer. *Enciclopedia culinaria confitería y repostería.* Madrid: Espasa Calpe, 2003.

de Leon, Josefina Velázquez. *La cocina económica, quinta edición.* Mexico City, Mexico: Editorial Velázquez de León, 1962.

de Medina, María R. *Helados pasteles y dulces.* Mexico City, Mexico: Medina Hermanos, 1973.

del Paso, Socorro and Fernando del Paso. *La cocina Mexicana.* Mexico City, Mexico: Punto de Lectura, 1991.

"El Dulce en México." *Artes de México,* 16: 121. Foto Ilustradores, 1969.

Fiscal, María Rosa. *Sabores de Durango.* Mexico City, Mexico: Conaculta, 2005.

Garcia, Rogelio Morales. *Pátzcuaro: cuna de la patria y esplendor del cielo.* Morelia, Mexico: Ediciones Mich, 2006.

Jacob, Dianne. *Will Write for Food.* New York: Marlowe and Company, 2005.

Jaén, Anina Jimeno. *El sabor de las palabras.* Mexico City, Mexico: Santillana Ediciones Generales, 2008.

Kennedy, Diana. *The Cuisines of Mexico.* New York: Harper/Row, 1972.

Mejía, Jairo. *Cocina Méxicana del siglo XIX.* Editorial Trillas, 2002.

Mintz, Sidney W. *Sabor a comida, sabor a libertad: incursiones en la comida, la cultura y el pasado,* Mexico City, Mexico: Ediciones de la Reina Roja, 2003.

Novo, Salvador. *Historia gastronómica de la ciudad de México,* Mexico City, Mexico: Editorial Porrua, 1972.

Puig, Jose Soler. *El pan dormido,* Havana, Cuba: Ediciones Huracán, 1977.

Rosell, Juan Pablo and Elba Castromex. *Cocinar en Jalisco.* Mexico City, Mexico: Landucci Editores, 2003.

Stoopen, Maria. *El universo de la cocina Mexicana.* Mexico City, Mexico: Fomento Cultural Banamex, 1988.

Stoopen, María. *La cocina Veracruzana.* Mexico City, Mexico: Artes Gráficas Panorama, 1992.

Yturbide, Teresa Castelló and María Josefa Martínez del Rio de Redo. *Delicias de antaño: historia y recetas de los conventos mexicanos.* Mexico City, Mexico: Landucci Editores, 2000.

Zurita, Ricardo Muñoz. *Diccionario enciclopédico de gastronomía Mexicana,* Mexico City: Editorial Clio, 2000.

INDEX

Published in the United States by Ten Speed Press,
an imprint of the Crown Publishing Group,
a division of Random House, Inc., New York.
www.crownpublishing.com
www.tenspeed.com

Ten Speed Press and the Ten Speed Press colophon are registered trademarks of Random House, Inc.

Library of Congress Cataloging-in-Publication Data

Gerson, Fany.
   My sweet Mexico : recipes for authentic breads, pastries, candies,
beverages, and frozen treats / Fany Gerson. — 1st ed.
      p. cm.
   Includes bibliographical references and index.
   Summary: "The first cookbook to present authentic versions of beloved Mexican sweets plus a creative selection of new recipes rooted in traditional flavors and ingredients—Provided by publisher.
1. Desserts—Mexico. 2. Cookery, Mexican. I. Title.
   TX773.G3823 2010
   641.5972—dc22

                          2010014469

ISBN: 978-1-58008-994-4

Printed in China

Design by Katy Brown

10 9 8 7 6 5 4 3 2 1

First Edition

A mi pa . . . por las alas

MEASUREMENT CONVERSION CHARTS

Volume

U.S.	IMPERIAL	METRIC
1 tablespoon	½ fl oz	15 ml
2 tablespoons	1 fl oz	30 ml
¼ cup	2 fl oz	60 ml
⅓ cup	3 fl oz	90 ml
½ cup	4 fl oz	120 ml
⅔ cup	5 fl oz (¼ pint)	150 ml
¾ cup	6 fl oz	180 ml
1 cup	8 fl oz (⅓ pint)	240 ml
1¼ cups	10 fl oz (½ pint)	300 ml
2 cups (1 pint)	16 fl oz (⅔ pint)	480 ml
2½ cups	20 fl oz (1 pint)	600 ml
1 quart	32 fl oz (1⅔ pint)	1 l

Weight

U.S./IMPERIAL	METRIC
½ oz	15 g
1 oz	30 g
2 oz	60 g
¼ lb	115 g
⅓ lb	150 g
½ lb	225 g
¾ lb	350 g
1 lb	450 g

Temperature

Fahrenheit	Celsius/Gas Mark
250°F	120°C/gas mark ½
275°F	135°C/gas mark 1
300°F	150°C/gas mark 2
325°F	160°C/gas mark 3
350°F	180 or 175°C/gas mark 4
375°F	190°C/gas mark 5
400°F	200°C/gas mark 6
425°F	220°C/gas mark 7
450°F	230°C/gas mark 8
475°F	245°C/gas mark 9
500°F	260°C

Length

INCH	METRIC
¼ inch	6 mm
½ inch	1.25 cm
¾ inch	2 cm
1 inch	2.5 cm
6 inches (½ foot)	15 cm
12 inches (1 foot)	30 cm